THE ESSENTIAL
NOSTRADAMUS

To 'The Man from the East'

THE ESSENTIAL

NOSTRADAMUS

PROPHECIES FOR THE 21ST CENTURY AND BEYOND

John Hogue

vega

ISBN 1-84333-597-2

A catalogue record for this book is available
from the British Library

Published in 2002 by
Vega
64 Brewery Road
London, N7 9NT

A member of **Chrysalis** Books plc

Visit our website at www.chrysalisbooks.co.uk

Printed in Great Britain
by Butler & Tanner Ltd, Frome and London

CONTENTS

INTRODUCTION:
THE LIFE AND WORK OF NOSTRADAMUS

CHAPTER I
PROPHECIES FROM THE PAST

CHAPTER II
PROPHECIES FOR THE PRESENT DAY AND THE NEAR FUTURE

CHAPTER III
PROPHECIES FOR THE FAR DISTANT FUTURE

Phœnix

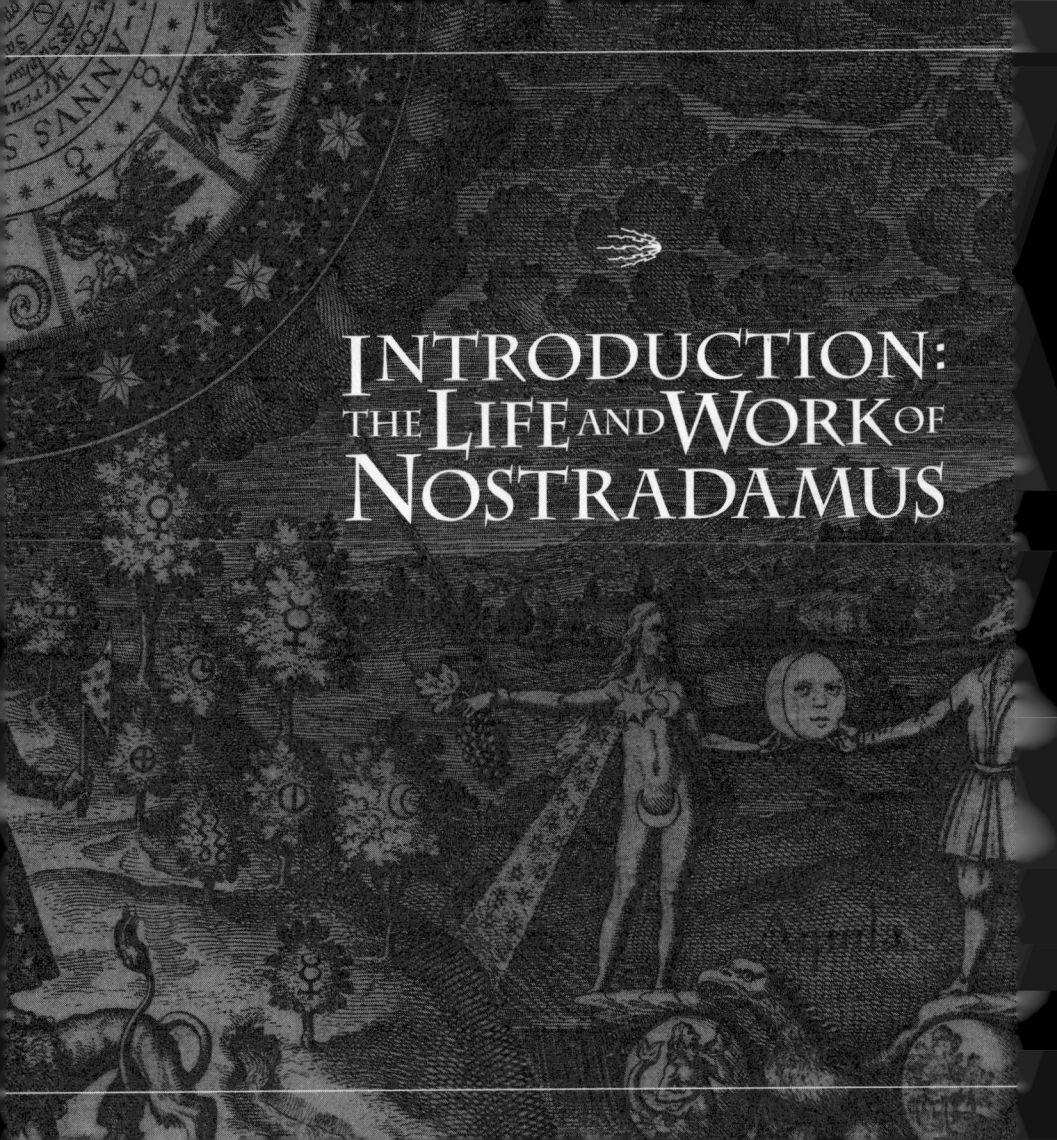

INTRODUCTION:
THE LIFE AND WORK OF
NOSTRADAMUS

DISTILLING THE DIVINER

*

Nostradamus casts his giant shadow on the world of prophecy as the genre's greatest failure. Not because his 1,477 predictions were wrong. This 16th-century doctor, herbalist and Renaissance man accurately foresaw many of the important figures and defining events and calamities of the last 445 years. He saw the coming of the French and Russian Revolutions. He named Louis Pasteur outright and dated his groundbreaking discoveries in medicine. Nostradamus described men walking on the moon and falling from the skies in the *Challenger* space shuttle disaster. He saw Napoleon and Hitler, the world wars and the global village that followed with the human race of that far-off time (our time) flying through the air 'over mountains, continents and oceans'. Nevertheless, he failed in his mission as a prophet because we continue not to heed his warnings.

Perhaps the sheer volume of his 36,000 words of warning tend to overwhelm those who might gain insight and help prevent the dangerous potential events that are coming. Our fast-paced time of fast food and fast facts requires the creation of a pocket book that briefly and comprehensively gives the reader of this travail-full new millennium the essential view of things to come.

The Essential Nostradamus will take you through a fundamental examination of the master prophet's life and magical practices used to see tomorrow. After a short review of the dos and don'ts of decoding Nostradamus' symbolic language, we then plunge through a few dozen of his most chilling and clear prophetic successes. Finally, we make a great leap forward into an indispensable exploration of the nightmares and hopes of the new millennium and beyond.

THE LIFE OF NOSTRADAMUS

FAMILY BACKGROUND

Michel de Nostredame was born in 1503 to recently 'Christianized' Jews in the town of St Rémy, Provence, yet scholars still debate over his family's true background and economic status. Some believe he was the son of a Jewish grain dealer called Jaume, while others say his father was a prosperous notary by the name of Jacques.

Michel's mysterious talent for prophecy was first encouraged by his grandfathers who took turns being his tutor. They were both learned men of the Renaissance, who in younger days were the personal physicians to the most free-thinking king of the time, Réné the Good of Provence, and his son, the Duke of Calabria. Their eager pupil showed a superior aptitude for mathmatics and the celestial science of astrology.

EDUCATION

His paternal grandfather deemed him ready at 14 to study liberal arts at Avignon, the papal enclave of Provence. At 19 he was sent to study medicine at the University of Montpellier (although some scholars dispute the timing and believe he spent the following nine years roaming S.W. France, learning directly from life his legendary skills as a herbalist and free-style apothecary). If the former story is correct then our young and gifted medical student breezed through his baccalaureate examinations in 1525. Soon afterwards an outbreak of bubonic plague disrupted his schooling for a few years. Sixteenth-century France suffered from seasonal bouts of *le Charbon*, the figurative description of the day for the carbon-black pustules of the black death. So severe was this new outbreak that the University of Montpellier closed its doors, and faculty and students alike fanned out through southern France to battle the disease. With a licence to practise medicine in hand, Michel de Nostredame saddled up his mule, packed his medical and astrological books and astrolabe, and set off on the open road on the trail of the plague. The emergency had liberated him from the fundamentally primitive views of his teachers and provided the freedom to put his medical theories to the test.

THE YOUNG PLAGUE DOCTOR

Whatever Nostradamus was by 1525 – either a freelance apothecary, or one licensed to practise medicine, if not yet a degreed physician – he followed the plague's shadow westwards through Montpellier, Narbonne, Toulouse, and all the way to Bordeaux, never leaving a town until the danger had passed. He honed his skills and availed himself of the knowledge and teachers of the Counter-Reformation's mystical underground of alchemists, Moorish medicine men, Jewish Cabalists, and pagans. His understanding of the importance of hygiene was quite progressive and controversial for the times. By 1529 he returned to Montpellier, where he received his doctorate and adopted the Latinized name *Nostradamus*. He remained a professor of medicine there for the following three years until friction over the rigid and conservative curriculum became unbearable for him and he left to set up a practice in Toulouse.

THE RISE AND FALL OF DR. NOSTRADAMUS

In 1534 he moved to Agen, where he became friends with the volatile Julius-César Scaliger, one of the great minds of the Renaissance. In Agen Nostradamus fell in love and married Adriète de Loubéjac. Sceptics theorize that sympathetic biographers mistook the name of Nostradamus' bride for that of Scaliger's beautiful 16-year-old wife, whose name was Andriète de Roques-Lobéjac. We do know she bore him a beautiful boy and girl and for the next three years Nostradamus eased into an idyllic family life and a flourishing medical practice.

In 1537, tragedy struck with such brutal intensity that it nearly shattered the young doctor's spiritual and mental health. In that year the plague returned to Agen and his wife and children were among its first victims. Friends and family turned against him, holding him responsible for their deaths. Scaliger, who was prone to violent argument and breaking his friendships, chose this moment to castigate the young doctor. His wife's family sued him for their dead daughter's dowry and won. His patients abandoned him, since their superstition convinced them that a doctor who could not save his own family must be in league with the devil.

Next came the Church authorities, who questioned his making chance remarks years before. He had seen an inept workman making a bronze statue of the Virgin Mary and commented that he was 'casting demons'. After receiving the summons to face the Inquisition at Toulouse, Nostradamus packed a few belongings and stole away on his mule into the night.

THE PILGRIMAGE TO PRESCIENCE

History's account of the next six years of his life is vague and often apocryphal. We know he travelled as far north as Lorraine, as far east as Venice, and lived for a time as far south as Sicily. One can suppose that he wandered through western and southern Europe to avoid the Church Inquisitors, while trying to pick up the shattered pieces of his life with a pilgrimage of self-discovery. It is during this dark night of Nostradamus' wandering soul that the first legends of his awakening prophetic powers began to emerge.

A group of Franciscan monks travelling one day along a muddy road near the Italian town of Ancona suddenly saw the solitary doctor walking towards them.

As they approached he stood aside to let them pass, but on seeing Brother Felice Peretti he immediately bowed, then knelt in the mud before him. The friars, knowing that Peretti had previously been a swineherd and was of lowly birth, were puzzled by this homage and asked Nostradamus to explain. He replied: 'I must yield myself and bend a knee before His Holiness.'

The friars chuckled under their cassock hoods at the explanation but, 40 years after his chance meeting and nearly 20 years after the death of Nostradamus, Brother Peretti became Pope Sixtus V.

Another legend chronicles Nostradamus' stay at the château of Lord de Florinville while, on a stroll with his host around the grounds, the conversation turned to prophecy. Florinville wanted to put the prophet's powers to the test. They had stopped before an enclosure containing two suckling pigs, one black, one white. When Florinville asked Nostradamus which pig would provide dinner that night, he replied without hesitation, 'We will eat the black pig, but a wolf will eat the white.'

Florinville secretly ordered his cook to slaughter the white pig. The cook dressed the pig for the spit and left the kitchen on an errand, forgetting to close the door. On his return, he found Florinville's pet wolf cub happily devouring the white pig. The horrified man shooed it away and ran to the enclosure to fetch the black pig.

At dinner that night all mouths watered as the cook set the roasted pig before Lord Florinville, who smiled at

Nostradamus across the table.

'We are not eating the black pig as you predicted. And no wolf will touch it here.'

Nostradamus was so adamant that this was the black pig that Lord Florinville eventually summoned the cook. The cook admitted everything under the penetrating gaze of Nostradamus' grey eyes.

THE PLAGUE DOCTOR RETURNS

Nostradamus returned to the South of France in 1544, and set up medical practice in Marseilles. In the winter of 1544–45, Provence suffered one of its worst floods on record. By spring the rains and floodwaters receded, leaving one of the most devastating pestilences of the

Nostradamus abhorred
the treatment of plague
in the 16th century

century in their wake. Hysteria and death spread through most of southern France for several years. In 1546, the city fathers of Aix-en-Provence summoned Nostradamus to the afflicted capital of Provence to combat a severe outbreak of *le Charbon*. Nostradamus worked around the clock for the next 270 days ministering to the sick.

With the assistance of an apothecary named Joseph Turel Mercurin, Nostradamus produced fragrant herbal and rose-petal lozenges. He admonished his patients to always keep these 'rose pills' under their tongues without swallowing them. Other surviving fragments of his medical journals imply that, as much as possible, he avoided bleeding his plague patients. Nostradamus advised patients to make sure their drinking water and bedding were clean, and to open the windows of their foul-smelling bedrooms to fresh air. He suggested they eat a balanced diet low in animal fat and get a moderate amount of exercise. These regimens of diet, exercise and hygiene, along with his legendary health and fearlessness when facing disease, may have helped more to cure his patients than the rose pills themselves.

Once the danger had passed, the city parliament gave Nostradamus a pension for life and the citizens of Aix showered him with gratitude and awards. It is said that he gave many of the gifts to the families and dependants of those he had not been able to save.

The hero of Aix next received a call for help from

the city fathers of Salon. He had no sooner cured the plague there when he received an urgent call from Lyons. The city records cite him for controlling an outbreak of whooping cough through mass prescriptions filled by one pharmacist René Hepiliervard.

A New Life

Nostradamus returned to Salon in 1547 to settle there for the rest of his life. He was enchanted by the little town's beauty and dry, sunny skies. He stayed at the house of his brother, Bertrand de Nostredame. Bertrand is purported by some biographers to have introduced Nostradamus to an attractive and intelligent young woman of a wealthy and respected Salonoise family. The untimely death of a certain Jean Baulne would soon make the widow, Anne Ponsarde Gemelle, the new bride of the middle-aged Dr. Nostradamus.

For the next eight years Nostradamus gradually withdrew from medical practice to engage himself in a highly successful cosmetics cottage industry with the help of his wife.

WRITING A HISTORY OF THE FUTURE

From 1548 onwards, Dr. Nostradamus plunged whole-heartedly into the occult. He transformed a room in the top floor of his house into a secret study, and by 1550 started publishing an annual almanac that made a few cautious stabs at prediction. He was so encouraged by the reaction to his prophecies that he embarked on an ambitious project: the future history of the world, told in 1,000 enigmatic quatrains (four-line poems), using a mixture of French, Latin, Italian, Hebrew, Arabic and Greek.

He began work on *Les Propheties* on the night of Good Friday 1554. He planned to compose a total of ten volumes, or 'Centuries', of one hundred quatrains each.

He published the first three centuries in May 1555. They open with a Preface dedicated to his infant son, César. This letter contained confessions and descriptions of his prophetic techniques and a prose prophecy, that stretched his vision all the way to the year A.D. 3797. Nostradamus cranked out Centuries 4 to 7 by 1557. Incomplete editions survive of the last of these. He finished and published the final three centuries in 1557 and 1558, along with an ambitious prose prophecy letter, known as the *Epistle to Henry II*, written in a macabre and psychedelic prose rivalling the Book of Revelation. His publisher printed special copies of the Epistle and last 300 quatrains that found their way to French Court, but it was Nostradamus' wish to delay general publication until after his death to protect his growing family – Nostradamus and Anne would eventually have six children – from the mounting popularity and controversy of his prophecies.

NOTORIOUS FAME

By 1556 Nostradamus' *Les Propheties* was the rage at court. After her ladies-in-waiting showed Queen Catherine de' Medici a *quatrain* predicting the death of her husband, King Henry II, in a jousting accident, she had Nostradamus summoned to Paris. His royal audience was a success and he became an intimate friend to the queen. Nostradamus was back in Salon when Henry II fulfilled that prophecy in 1559. This was the first of several successful predictions fulfilled in his own lifetime that would make Nostradamus' prophecies the talk of the courts of Europe.

Persecution followed fame. During the early 1560s, France was lurching towards the first of nine civil wars fought over religion and street ruffians began tormenting Nostradamus in Salon. Though he outwardly practised Catholicism, many Catholics viewed the Christianized Jew as a Calvinist heretic, while the Protestants and Calvinists of Salon cursed him as a papist.

Greater dangers also attracted greater supporters to his name. The Duke and Duchess of Savoy became his patrons. It is said he cast an accurate astrological forecast for their newborn son, who later became Savoy's most remarkable ruler, Charles-Emmanuel 'the Great'. It is during this time that Nostradamus played with writing Centuries 11 and 12, but only fragments remain. From 1550 until his death he continued to compose highly popular annual almanacs containing prose prognostications, and later, annual bundles of quatrains predicting the events of the coming year.

HONOURED IN HIS FINAL DAYS

In 1564, while on a tour of appeasement through the French realm, Catherine de' Medici (now the Queen Regent) and the adolescent King Charles IX made a point of visiting the ageing prophet of Salon. Before resuming their tour, Catherine had Charles IX honour Nostradamus with the title Counsellor and Physician in Ordinary, with the privileges and salary this implied.

Nostradamus reached the high point of his

prophetic career with only a year and eight months left to live. His noted robust health underwent a rapid collapse by mid-1566. In June, upon returning from the royal Embassy of Arles as a representative of the king, Nostradamus had a severe attack of gout, which soon developed into dropsy (pulmonary oedema). He asked his family and disciples to move his deathbed into his beloved secret study where, in great physical pain, but spiritual serenity, he awaited his end. His last prediction concerned his own approaching death:

On his return from the Embassy, the king's gift put in place. He will do nothing more, He will be gone to God. Close relatives, friends, brothers by blood (will find him) completely dead near the bed and the bench.

At daybreak on 2 July 1566, family and friends found him dead in his bed with his swollen leg propped on a bench, exactly as he predicted.

Anne carried out her husband's final request that his coffin should be standing upright, enclosed within an inside wall of the Church of the Cordeliers of Salon.

ANGELS, DAEMONS AND DIVINATION

✸

A good magician never reveals the full nature of his secrets. At best we only have Nostradamus' hints at the magical route he took to unlock the future.

Nostradamus' various confessions on the matter hint at his prophetic power coming from God. The mortal prophet receives messages carried down through a relay consisting of a hierarchy of spirits. Nostradamus, standing in his magic circle in his secret study, may have used ancient Cabalistic techniques to conjure good angels rather than the more elemental and lower denizens of the astral plane known as *daemons*.

In his prophecies he speaks of divine ones, or angels, that sit at his side when he is deep in trance. They reveal to him what he calls a 'prophetic heat' and vision. This divine fire of prophecy descends upon the prophet's stilled mind and heart like the brilliance of the sun. It guides the spectral emissaries to influence the mortal medium to prophesy.

Nostradamus' Bible of Magic

Nostradamus' occult confessions reveal his heavy reliance on the neo-Platonist magician Iamblichus (died, A.D. 330). He no doubt had a copy of Marsilio Ficino's translation of Iamblichus' *De mysteriis Aegyptiorum*, the bible on Egyptian, Chaldaean and Assyrian magic rituals that is often cited in Nostradamus' confessions about his magic rituals. Nostradamus also relied on the occult works attributed to the biblical King Solomon, and a rare treatise in Greek by the noted Byzantine historian, Michael Psellus (1018–78), entitled *Of Daemons According to the Dogma of the Greeks*.

Nostradamus' Philosophy on Time

If we take his studies of classical divination as an indicator, it is safe to say that Nostradamus believed that the divine world of eternity contains all the potential destinies, causes and effects, and archetypes expressed in the physical, time-

The great Nostradamus
employed many techniques
for divination

bound world. A mortal man, by nature, is limited to the rules of time and space. His sense of time is linear. He is like a man at the fork of a crossroads who cannot look beyond the horizon of the present to see which road is the right one to travel. But through magical meditations, and with the assistance of divine messengers and lower elemental spirits, he can enter within himself to access the invisible, latent flame of divinity sleeping within everyone. For brief moments he can tap into the divine ecstasy of the 'Ever Now' state of eternity, and from this higher state of awareness, his soul can gaze down at the same crossroads stretching beyond the physical present and see potential future events on various paths of destiny radiating from the present. It is as if these divine spirits, in union with his own expanded consciousness, take him to a much higher vibration from where he can view the faraway bumps and turns down the crossroads of destiny.

HOW THE PROPHET PREPARED HIMSELF TO SEE THE FUTURE

We can surmise that a nocturnal session would have Nostradamus prepare himself by fasting for three days to disconnect from the corporeal energies of the body. He would also abstain from sex to build his psychic energies and direct them upwards towards the ethereal plane. Night is preferable for the conjuration of spirits. The weather should not be stormy, too windy or disturbed by the shadows of moving clouds. A magician must take great care to astrologically plot the right hour for conjuring each specific class of spirit messenger: the archangels, angels, heroes and elemental daemons.

Before entering his secret study he would bathe himself in consecrated water, don a simple robe and take up a laurel branch as his magic wand. He would enter a consecrated circle drawn in the centre of the wooden floor and perhaps illuminated by candles. The circle protected him from the divine emissaries about to be conjured. His writings admit to a preference for angelic and daemonic messengers of fire and their different qualities of divine, non-physical light, although the works of Iamblichus and King Solomon also describe the invocation of spirits of water, earth, air and ether.

Nostradamus loved the hot and dry climate of his native Provence; perhaps he had his best success with the 'fiery missives' of angelic spirits.

Our prophet sits upon a tripod over which a brass bowl is filled to the brim with steaming water made pungent with stimulating oils and perhaps lightly narcotic herbs. This is done to imitate the volcanic fissure the priestess of Ancient Greece (known as the Oracle of Delphi) imbibed to prepare for her possession by a god so that she could predict the future. Between deep inhalations of perfumed vapour he, like the oracle, chants magic incantations and feels the minute flame of divine fire penetrate his soul. At the right moment, Nostradamus dips his wand into the brass bowl.

He anoints his foot and the hem of his robe. A sudden rush of paranormal energy into his body is at first frightening, but he surrenders himself to it and ecstasy transports him into a psychic trance. The voice of a higher entity vibrates inside him. He lowers a consecrated pen to parchment and begins to write a history of the future, as it is told by the hushed voice of his divine messenger.

THE DIVINATION TECHNIQUES OF NOSTRADAMUS

His incantations for spirit communication are mostly derived from the *Keys of Solomon*. It is possible he uttered them in Hebrew rather than Latin. The magical tools and disciplines he may have used within the circle to bring himself into a trance were varied, although most of them required the discipline of scrying – gazing on certain objects without blinking. Some believe he sat in his observatory gazing at the reflection of stars in a dark bowl of water. He used hydromancy extensively when in the magic circle of his study and to a lesser extent may have gazed at a flame or peered into the deep and polished surface of a lead or pewter mirror.

The most famous and controversial Assyrian technique comes from his study of Psellus, who wrote:

'Thus those about to prophesy take a basin full of water which attracts the spirits creeping stealthily in the depths. The basin then full of water (to the brim) seems… to breathe as

with sounds; it seems to me that the water was agitated with circular ripples as from some sound emitted below.

Now this water diffused through the basin differs but little in kind from water out of the basin, but yet it much excels it from a virtue imparted on it by the incantations which have rendered it more apt to receive the spirit of prophecy. For this description of spirit is peevish and earth-bound and much under the influence of composite spells.

When the water begins to lend itself as the vehicle of sound, the spirit also presently gives out a thin, reedy note but devoid of meaning; and close upon that, while the water is undulating, certain weak and peeping sounds whisper forth predictions of the future.'

How Nostradamus Set Down his Visions

At first light he would move from the magic circle over to his writing desk where he would get to work translating his visions into prose. He would pull out consecrated paper and write with a pen made from the third feather of the right wing of a white male gosling, ceremoniously plucked.

Only on the first rewrite would Nostradamus cloak his notes into obscure and coded four-line poems. He made sure the prophecies were out of sequence. Legend states that he wrote each quatrain on a single piece of paper and had Chavigny, his apprentice, toss them in the air to be gathered in whatever order they fell. Although many Nostradamians down through the centuries want to believe he hid his original notes for later discovery, it is more likely he consigned them to the flames of his alchemical furnace once the quatrains were written.

ASTROLOGY DISCIPLINES USED

Judicial astrology is known today as political astrology. It encompasses the plotting of astrology charts for countries, state leaders, and the birth of constitutions and governments. Nostradamus in his writings confesses that he used the discipline of judicial astrology to translate his fanciful visions into objective ideas for writing.

How to Decipher Nostradamus

❋

His writings tell us that Nostradamus consciously chose to write about the future in an obscure and calculatedly nebulous style so that the ignorant and prejudiced would deem him a fool and leave him alone, while the more open-minded might pass beyond the verbal roadblocks to glimpse future human potential for good and evil.

Nostradamus establishes some important ground rules:

1. He deals only with significant events that could – or did – change the course of history.

2. All the bad grammar, the enigmas, anagrams, the mix of several languages, the bald-faced absurdities and the general cloudiness of his writing are devices to hide truths from those who want the future to mould itself around their hopes and fears. It may even be done to hide the prophecies from future tyrants, who might recognize their mistakes in the prophecies, change their decisions and perhaps create a worse future than Nostradamus had foreseen. Imagine what would have happened if in 1990 Saddam Hussein had recognized himself in the prophecies and decided to attack Kuwait in 1996 after he tipped his missiles with nuclear weapons? A man who can see tomorrow has a great karmic responsibility.

3. Obscurity works as a pacifier. The mediocre-minded can project their ideas on Nostradamus' opacity and satisfy themselves that either he is a charlatan or he supports their fragile, or airy-fairy, sentiments.

Nostradamus hinted that he wrote his special prophetic language for the meek – or better, the 'humble' – in spirit, who are willing to move beyond their own conditioned and egoistic projections to experience Nostradamus' hidden secrets.

Before beginning a journey through time and our projections, it would be advisable to study some of Nostradamus' grammar rules and decoding techniques.

ANAGRAMS

Nostradamus scrambled words and phrases to construct other words and phrases using the same letters; for example: *rapis* becomes *Paris*. Nostradamus made his own variations for switching or replacing letters. One or two letters can be dropped; for example, letters can be added and/or changed: *Hister* becomes *Hitler*.

NO SEQUENCE OF TIME

The prophecies rarely follow any logical sequence. The events they describe are frequently scrambled out of chronological order – even within a quatrain itself – requiring the interpreter to find key phrases and words linking the events into some understandable order.

THE POLITICS OF ANIMAL NAMES

Countries are characterized as animals, in the form of heraldic or mystical symbols associated with a particular country. For example, *Cock* for France, *Bear* for Berlin or Russia, or *Wolf* for Italy.

PROPER NAMES IN UNCOMMON PLACES

Proper names can be hidden in normal French words and phrases and vice versa. Even verbs and adjectives can hide a name. *Abas*, meaning 'to put down', can stand for the future Antichrist *Mabus*, or for *Abbas*, a common Arabic name.

Insignias as Portents

You will see plays on words and phrases identifying people and movements through their insignias, coats of arms or other emblems.

Remote Viewing

Geographically speaking, the predictions that apply to France and its neighbours are clearer and more numerous than those about distant lands.

Alternative Futures

To the modern reader most of Nostradamus' predictions seem obscure tangles of syntax and jumbled meaning. Of his known 1,110 quatrains over 800 are little more than augury-babble. They may be just his prophetic mistakes, or perhaps some seem nonsensical to us because their details concern events in our unknown future. I believe many of the incomprehensible quatrains are accurate chronicles of events that might have been if history had taken a different turn – predictions for a parallel universe, even.

THE DIFFICULTY IN DECIPHERING NOSTRADAMUS

Nostradamus intentionally obscured his prophecies, setting the stage for interpreters to attempt untangling them for centuries to come. Whether a given interpretation for a quatrain is the one he intended or whether his wildly obscure crabbed poetry was meant to unlock the interpreter's own second sight cannot be resolved. The obscurity by its nature cannot prove or disprove that our interpretations of Nostradamus are the correct ones. Sometimes the commentators accurately foresee future events reflected in the prophet's obscurity even when their slant on a prophecy, in my opinion, was not aligned with Nostradamus' intent.

A deep and careful examination of his prophecies will reveal evidence supporting the argument that Nostradamus had many layers of intention for the use of his prophecies. One important one is that each generation can use them to see how the infinite potentials of the future reflect the positive and negative consequences of our present actions. If we can correctly interpret these potentials they can help us change ourselves for the better, *today*, because we can never live in the future. It has always been and it will always be *today*.

Phœnix.

CHAPTER I
PROPHECIES FROM THE PAST

※

Nostradamus wrote over a thousand
predictions. These are a few examples
of his hundreds of prophetic successes.

The Jeane Dixon of the 16th Century:
PREDICTING THE DEATH OF HENRY II

Le lyon ieune le vieux furmontera,
En champ bellique par fingulier duelle:
Dans caige d'or les yeux luy creuera,
Deux claffes vne, puis mourir, mort cruelle.

The young lion will overcome the older one
On the field of combat in single battle:
He will pierce his eyes through a golden cage
Two wounds made one, then he dies a cruel death.

(Century 1 : Quatrain 35) [1]

The quatrains foretelling the death of King Henry II of France in a jousting accident is one of the most famous, pre-documented and successfully fulfilled prophecies in history. It has only one comparable parallel to our time. In the 1950s American psychic, Jeane Dixon, documented accurate forecasts of the rise of John F. Kennedy to the presidency and his assassination.

At the end of June 1559, Henry II ignored all warnings coming from Nostradamus and others against participating in ritual combat and decided to celebrate the dual marriage of his sister Marguerite to the Duke of Savoy, and his daughter Elizabeth by proxy to King Philip II of Spain, by staging a three-day tournament along the rue St Antoine outside Paris. On the final day the king, resplendent in full gilded armour and wielding a great lion-decorated shield, had demanded one more unscheduled match with the Gabriel de Lorge, the Comte de Montgomery.

Upon his next charge down the lists a great splinter of ragged wood from Montgomery's lance rammed through the king's gilded visor and he fell mortally wounded.

Both men that day held shields embossed with lions. Montgomery was six years younger than Henry, who was 41. A tournament is a *field of* ritual *single combat*. During the final bout Montgomery failed to drop his lance in time. It shattered, sending a large splinter through the king's gilded visor *(golden cage)*.

Henry suffered two mortal wounds. One splinter destroyed the king's eye, another impaled his temple just behind the eye; both penetrated his brain *(two wounds made one)*. He lingered for ten agonizing days *(then he dies a cruel death)*.

[1] Indexing for prophecies taken from Nostradamus' work *Les Propheties*: 1 (Century/Volume) Q (Quatrain number) 35

THE FRENCH REVOLUTION:
THE FLIGHT TO VARENNES

De nuict viendra par la foreſt de Reines,
Deux pars vaultorte Herne la pierre blanche:
Le moine noir en gris dedans Varennes,
Eſleu Cap, cauſe tempeſte, feu, ſang tranche.

By night he will come by the forest of Reines,
A married couple, devious route, Queen white stone:
A monk-king in grey in Varennes,
Elected Cap, causes tempest, fire, and bloody slicing.

(Century 9 : Quatrain 20)

On the night of 20 June 1791, King Louis XVI and the French royal family, disguised as servants of Baroness de Korff, left Paris in a heavy covered carriage to journey north to the border in a failed attempt to escape the French Revolutionaries.

Over two centuries before this doomed escape attempt and its tragic consequences were played out, Nostradamus had foreseen it all.

This quatrain is startlingly accurate in every detail. Its index number 20 stands for the date of the attempted escape – 20 June 1791. The royal family's road to freedom took them past the *forest of Reines*, but poor roads and a lack of replacement horses eventually forced their coach to make a time-consuming detour. *Devious*

...Queen white stone: A monk-king in grey
in Varennes, Elected Cap, causes tempest,
fire, and bloody slicing. (9 Q20)

thus describes a detour, the secrecy and their disguise. Witnesses who reported seeing the pair during their escape described them as a *married couple* and others believed Louis was a monk. The town of *Varennes* was the scene of their discovery. *Queen white stone* gives in only three words a perfect description of Marie Antoinette's appearance and emotional state: she wore a white dress, and some said that shock and distress turned her hair white. *White stone* could be a double-pun alluding both to her hardness of heart towards the lower classes and lack of personal warmth, and to her involvement in a notorious diamond necklace scandal prior to the Revolution. *Elected Cap*, is Louis Capet, the commoner's name used by the former supreme ruler

Louis XVI when he was made the *elected* monarch of the new constitutional government. His execution (*causes tempest*) sparks a counter-revolution that will be suppressed by the Republicans with the blade of the guillotine (*bloody slicing*).

THE DOCTOR PROPHET NAMES A FUTURE MEDICAL GIANT

Perdu trouué, caché de ſi long ſiecle,
Sera Paſteur demy Dieu honoré:
Ains que la Lune acheue ſon grand ſiecle,
Par autres vents fera deshonoré.

The lost thing is found, hidden for so many centuries,
Pasteur will be honoured as a demigod:
This happens when the moon completes her great cycle,
He will be dishonoured by other rumours as foul as farting.

(Century 1 : Quatrain 25)

To combat the plague, Nostradamus used medical techniques that were centuries ahead of his time. One prophecy in particular has caused much speculation as to whether the 16th-century doctor used his prophetic skills to save lives.

Louis Pasteur's discovery that germs pollute the atmosphere was one of the greatest milestones in medical history, and contemporaries called him a *demigod*. Until his theories were proved beyond doubt, he endured vicious attacks from influential colleagues in the medical academies of his time. Nostradamus not only names Pasteur, but the prophet also correctly dated the establishment of the *Institut Pasteur*. He achieved this by reference to the last great lunar cycle in astrology, which began in 1535 and ended in 1889, the year the institute was created.

A century after his death in 1895, a new scandal threatens Pasteur's posterity. Princeton historian Gerald Geison, in his book *The Private Science of Louis Pasteur*, finds a self-serving and sloppy scientist hiding behind this legend of scientific discovery and altruism. His source is a careful reading of Pasteur's original lab books. Pasteur's notes do show that he tested his rabies vaccine on a nine-year-old boy bitten by a rabid dog, as is popularly believed, but they also overturn his public claim that he had done thorough tests before making a child his lab mouse for experimental treatments. Whether Pasteur will be *dishonoured* or

Geison's book will be viewed as *foul rumours* is left for the future to decide.

FRANCE WAS WARNED OF NAZI INVASION BUT NO ONE LISTENED

Pres du grand fleuue, grand foffe, terre egefte,
En quinze pars sera l'eau diuifee:
La cité prinfe, feu, fang, cris conflict mettre,
Et la plus part concerne au collifee.

Near the great river, a vast trench, earth excavated,
It will be divided by water into fifteen parts:
The city taken, fire, blood, cries and battle given,
The greater part involving the collision [*of forces*].

(Century 4 : Quatrain 80)

Before World War II, the French government and its military advisors steadfastly believed that the great eastern underground network of fortifications, called the Maginot Line, was impregnable. Its very existence led to a false sense of security.

Half the fortifications faced the *great river* Rhine. The Maginot Line was broken in 15 places by rivers. No other eastern defensive trench in history can claim this feature.

The city in the quatrain is Paris, taken as a result of a sudden *collision* of battles fought by German panzers who sidestepped the Maginot Line to break through French and British forces in Belgium, then plunged deep into France to seize the exposed French capital.

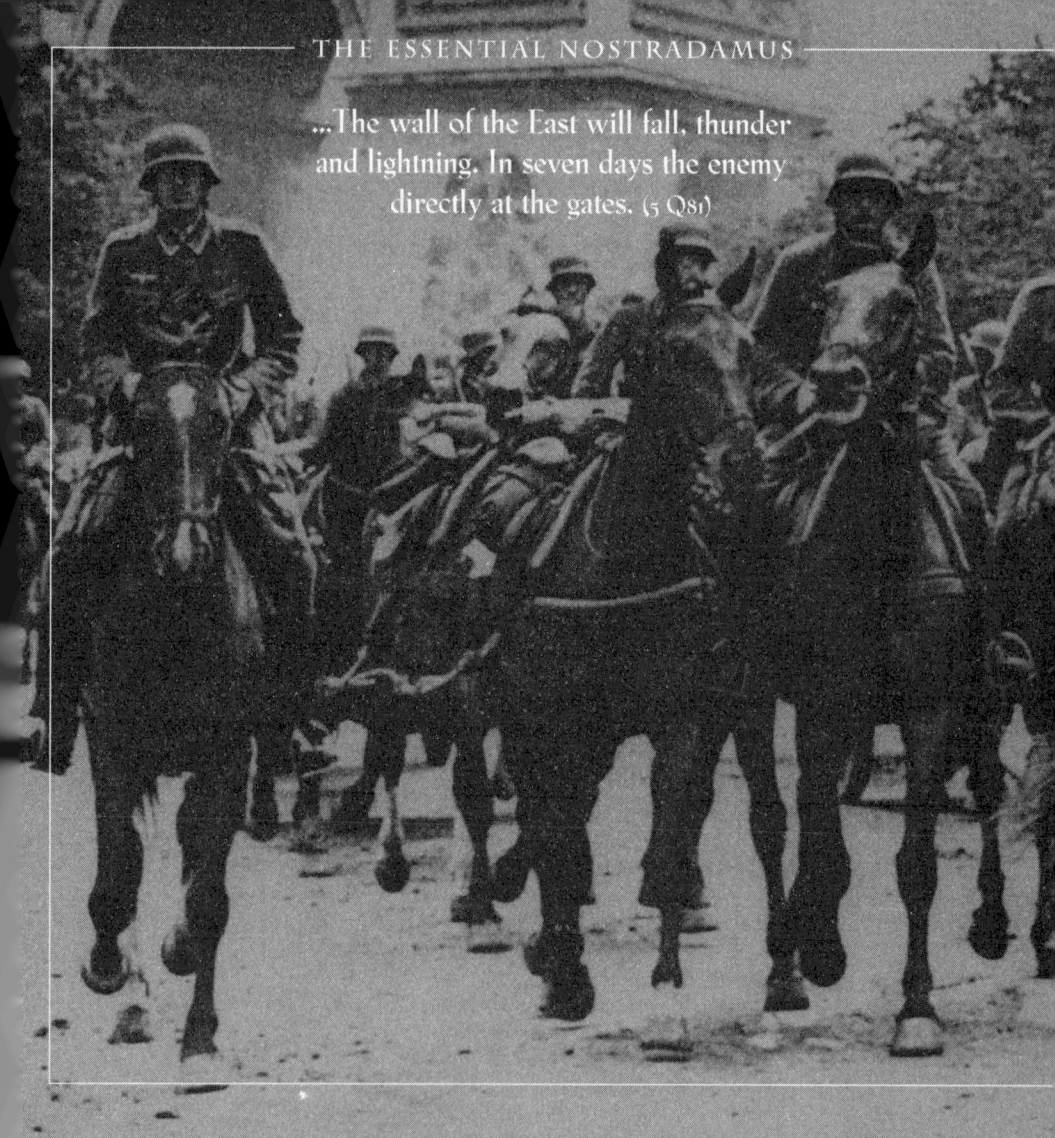

...The wall of the East will fall, thunder and lightning. In seven days the enemy directly at the gates. (5 Q81)

Et tranflaté pres d'arduenne filue... (5 Q45)

...Qu'il mettra foudres, combien en tel arroy,
Peu & loing puis profond és Hefperiques. (4 Q99)

...Mur d'Orient cherra tonnerre efclaire,
Sept iours aux portes les ennemis à l'heure. (5 Q81)

...Near the forest of the Ardennes. (5 Q45)

...He will launch thunderbolts –
so many and in such an array
Near, and far, then deep into the West. (4 Q99)

...The wall of the East will fall, thunder and lightning.
In seven days the enemy directly at the gates. (5 Q81)

Hitler's panzer armies flanked the eastern wall of the Maginot Line with lightning thrusts through Flanders and a surprise thunder stroke through the Ardennes. After the British expeditionary force was evacuated at Dunkirk, Hitler's blitzkrieg (lightning war) turned southwest, plunging through France. The thrust to Paris took only seven days!

Beſtes farouches de faim fleuues tranner,
Plus part du champ encontre Hiſter ſera.
En caige de fer le grand fera treiſner,
Quand rien enfant de Germain obſeruera.

(*Century 2 : Quatrain 24*)

Beasts wild with hunger will cross the rivers,
The greater part of the battlefield will be against Hister.
Into a cage of iron will the great one be drawn,
When the child of Germany observes no law.

(Century 2 : Quatrain 24)

Europe's vast rivers became natural obstacles playing a major part in Hister's – or Hitler's – 'Fortress Europe' defence plan, especially on the Eastern Front. Titanic Soviet offensives crossed rivers: the Volga (Stalingrad, 1942), the Dnieper (Kiev, 1943), the Danube (Budapest, 1944), the Oder (Berlin, 1945); and in the Western Front British and American offensives cross the Rhine (Arhnem, 1944, and the Battle of the

Rhine, 1945). The final line describes the madness that befell Germany under the Third Reich. From its inception, a majority of its children were members of the Hitler Youth, which had as its major goal the reprogramming of the minds of German children to become good 'barbarians'.

MAN WILL WALK ON THE MOON AND FALL FROM THE SKY

Dedans le coing de Luna viendra rendre,
Ou fera prins & mis en terre eftrange,
Les fruicts immeurs feront à grand efclandre
Grand vitupere à l'vn grande louange.

He will come to take himself to the corner of the Moon,
Where he will be taken and placed on alien land,
The unripe fruit will be the source of great scandal,
Great blame, to the other great praise.

(Century 9 : Quatrain 65)

Nostradamus dared to propose that someday men would be able to walk upon another planet. The last two lines could bring us back down to Earth to the *Challenger* disaster. The American space programme was castigated for sending their astronauts on the *unripe fruit* of faulty rocket boosters prematurely approved to fit the budget. At the time of the *Challenger* disaster, however, the Soviet space programme was running smoothly with the complete support of its government and people (*to the other great praise*).

D'humain troupeau neuf feront mis à part,
De iugement & confeil feparez:
Leur fort fera diuifé en depart,
Kappa, Thita, Lambda, mors bannis efgarez.

...The unripe fruit will be the
source of great scandal, Great blame,
to the other great praise.

(9 Q65)

Nine will be set apart from the human flock
Separated from judgment and counsel:
Their fate to be determined on departure.
Kappa [*K*], Thita [*TH*], Lambda [*L*] dead,
banished and scattered.

(Century 1 : Quatrain 81)

On 28 January 1986, 71 seconds after lift-off, the United
States space shuttle *Challenger* exploded. In an era when
space flight would have been the stuff of fairy tales to
Nostradamus, apart from a mistake in numbers – nine
rather than seven killed – he makes an uncannily
accurate description of this disaster.

During the months of investigation following the
explosion, the National Aeronautics and Space

Administration (NASA) came under close scrutiny. The inquiry revealed flaws in the shuttle itself and in command decision-making (*separated from judgment and counsel*).

The final line, with its riddle of Greek letters could spell out the key player in the *Challenger* scandal: K, TH, L = (TH)io(K)o(L) = Thiokol. This could stand for the rocket manufacturer, Morton Thiokol Inc., which designed and built the faulty solid rocket boosters. In the scandal many company heads and engineers, along with a number of senior NASA officials, were fired (*banished and scattered*).

CHAPTER II
PROPHECIES FROM THE PRESENT DAY AND THE NEAR FUTURE

✳

One of the greatest popular misunderstandings
about the prophecies of Nostradamus is that
they foretell the end of the world for July 1999.
Well, if you are reading this today you know
how wrong that interpretation is. Indeed,
Nostradamus foresaw at least another 1,798
years of Earth history – and perhaps thousands
of years of extraterrestrial history – remaining
for humanity beyond 1999. Here are a few
of the finest examples of present-day
and near future prophecies.

THE KING OF TERROR IS REVEALED

L'an mil neuf cens nonante neuf sept mois,
Du ciel viendra vn grand Roy d'effrayeur.
Refusciter le grand Roy d'Angolmois.
Auant apres Mars regner par bon heur.

In the year 1999 and seven months,
The great King of Terror will come from the sky.
He will bring back Genghis Khan.
Before and after Mars rules happily.

(Century 10 : Quatrain 72)

Nostradamus' most famous doomsday prediction warns future generations of a *King of Terror* descending from the skies in July 1999. This holy terror could be Nostradamus' Third Antichrist who many interpreters thought would reveal himself in July 1999, and wage war on Israel or its Western allies *from the sky*, either with a nuclear missile or with a jet loaded with plutonium dust or chemical weapons detonated over a city. Since July 1999 came and went without much fanfare the supporters of this interpretation had to wait for July of the year 2000, because you can also translate the opening line's original French to mean you start counting the seven months at the end of 1999 – 'In the year 1999 *and* seven months' – or, July 2000.

Thus the Antichrist interpretation suffered strike two when no terrorist attacked in July 2000. Were the interpreters swinging at a non-existent prescient pitch? Line three metaphorically describes the time of the King of Terror's descent from the skies as the period when China becomes a superpower to rival America. It must be remembered that Genghis Khan, the great Mongol king, united the people of China and the Central Asian steppes into the world's first Sino-Islamic superpower. The vast Islamic western wing of his empire included modern-day Iraq, Iran, Pakistan and the Central Asian republics of the former Soviet Union, implying that a modern Genghis Khan and China might bring those nations again into its sphere of political and economic influence.

The phrase *before and after Mars rules happily* can be interpreted to mean that the higher occult aspect of Mars, as the god of magic and spiritual transformation, *rules happily* in the new millennium. The rise of China as a superpower to match America could bring either balance and stability to the world or a future world war. It all depends on which aspect we trigger by our actions.

Nostradamus often uses personifications to hide a phenomenon rather than a man, or vice versa. I believe the King of Terror is not the Antichrist. He or 'it' has already come – between July 1999 and July 2000 – and it is descending from our skies right now and will impact human civilization for the next 27 to 30 years.

The King of Terror is global warming.

The summer of 1999 saw a dramatic upswing in violent weather and abnormally high temperatures, signifying that our polluting of the atmosphere has so effectively trapped the Sun's heat that record-breaking temperature rises are a sign of things to come. It could be that the terror of a climate running out of control might be the cause of global stresses on food, water and economic sustainability. It may cause 'Mars' to rule 'happily' in its lower aspect of war and mayhem in some future conflict between China, the Middle East and America.

A GLOBAL DROUGHT OVER THE EARTH'S GRAIN BELTS

A quarante huict degré climaterique,
A fin de Cancer fi grande feichereffe:
Poiffon en mer, fleuue, lac cuit hectique,
Bearn, Bigorre par feu ciel en deftreffe.

At a latitude of the forty-eight degrees,
At the end of Cancer [*July 24th*] so great [*is the*] drought.
Fish in the sea, river and lake boiled hectic,
[*Southwest France*] in distress from fire in the sky.

(Century 5 : Quatrain 98)

...Fish in the sea, river and lake boiled
hectic, [*Southwest France*] in distress
from fire in the sky. (5 Q98)

The findings are in: the winter of 1999–2000 and 2001–02 were the hottest on record. The ice cap where one would stand over the North Pole has melted two years in a row. A piece of part of the Antarctic ocean ice shield the size of the American state of Delaware has broken up and released tens of thousands of ice shards into the southern oceans. The grain belts and Eastern Seaboard of North America are entering their fourth year of the greatest water shortage and drought in a century. A similar affliction befalls the grain belts of Siberia and Manchuria, causing 30,000 fires in the former, and dust storms over the latter that blot out the sun in China's capital, Beijing.

Scientists have traced the regularity of sunspot activity over the last billion years and relate it to 11-year cycles that coincide with periods of drought such as the one that created the infamous Dust Bowl. The *fire in the sky* from sunspot activity is now entering what some believe is a new 'Mega' cycle – a once-in-500-year explosion of solar activity lasting several years and bringing extreme weather and droughts.

Add to this our artificially produced global warming and Nostradamus warns us against creating a future drought of biblical proportions that will burn a swath across latitude 48 in the Northern Hemisphere. Drawing a line across that latitude on a map, we touch on nearly all the world's chief grain belts. If today's amber oceans of wheat stretching across North America, southwestern France, the Ukraine, Manchuria and Russia should revert to prairies and inhospitable steppes in a few decades, a global world war may arise not from religious or political differences but from the nations of Earth fighting over dwindling food and water resources.

GLOBAL FAMINE IS COMING! YOU HAVE BEEN WARNED

La grand famine que ie fens approcher,
Souuent tourner, puis eftre vniuerfelle:
Si grande & longue qu'un viendra arracher,
Du bois racine, & l'enfant de mammelle.

The great famine, which I sense approaching,
Will often turn [*up in various places*] then become universal:
It will be so vast and long lasting,
That [*people*] will grab roots from the trees
and children from the breast.

(Century 1 : Quatrain 67)

The 21st century has come. Each day 220,000 to 250,000 people are born, more than 100,000 new motor vehicles hit the road, we destroy more than 180 square miles of tropical rain forest, and an additional 60,000,000 metric tonnes of carbon dioxide contaminate the air.

The new millennium sees the exploding population ever more enamoured with the market-led, high-waste-producing American lifestyle, yet Worldwatch Institute reports our current global technologies and infrastructure and food sustainability can support a maximum worldwide population of only 2.5 billion living the American Dream. Maybe the 'King of Terror' came a little later than expected for July 1999. He is the sixth billionth child, born in October 1999. We will add a billion more ecologically harmful little terrors each 11 years. By 2020, China by itself could eat up the world, since it will require *all* the grain exports produced globally in the year 2000 to feed its children. By 2025, India, its neighbour, will run out of potable water. What will these nuclear powers do about their food and water problems then?

The plagues, famines and droughts predicted by Nostradamus have already begun and continue to be right on astrological schedule, as I correctly forecast in my first book in 1986. The growing world drought now sees half the current six billion people on Earth suffering from lack of adequate water. Crop yields cannot catch up with the demand of 80 to 90 million new mouths to feed each year. Tensions will rise, as will the threat of war.

> *L'an que Saturne & Mars efgaux combuſt,*
> *L'air fort feiché, longue traiection:*
> *Par feux fecrets, d'ardeur grand lieu aduſt*
> *Peu pluye, vent chault, guerres, incurſions.*

In the year when Saturn and Mars are equally fiery,
The air is very dry, a long comet:
From hidden fires a great place burns with heat,
Little rain, hot wind, wars and raids.

(Century 4 : Quatrain 67)

Here we have Nostradamus giving us astrological dates marking the spread of wars as a result of the stresses coming from a global drought and famine in the early 21st century. Saturn and Mars are *equally fiery* when they come together in an astrological fire sign – preferably one of those most responsible for wars and raids, Aries or Leo. Many 20th-century wars and military offensives parallel this aspect. Saturn joined Mars in Aries when Hitler's forces entered Warsaw in late September 1939, triggering World War II. In 1968, the Tet Offensive during the Vietnam conflict started with this conjunction of these planets in Aries.

Mars and Saturn in Leo coincide with catastrophes of civil unrest, such as during the Indian Partition of autumn 1947, when bloody riots and sectarian strife killed over one million Hindus and Muslims. In 1998 the conjunction of Mars and Saturn saw the *hot winds* of global warming coincide with the *wars and raids* during Serbia's ethnic cleansing of its Muslim citizens in Kosovo and NATO's air attacks on Serbia. We await other significant fiery transits of Mars with Saturn in Aries in 2026, and again in 2028. At that time the stresses of global warming and population may derail the human race in over 70 regional and civil wars.

9–11
THE ATTACK ON THE 'HOLLOW MOUNTAINS' OF NEW YORK

❋

Cinq & quarante degrés ciel bruflera,
Feu approcher de la grand cité neufue,
Inftant grand flamme efparfe fautera,
Quand on voudra des Normans faire preuue.

At forty–five degrees latitude, the sky will burn,
Fire approaches the great new city,
Immediately a huge, scattered flame leaps up,
When they want to have verification
from the Normans [*the French*].

(Century 6 : Quatrain 97)

The events of 11 September 2001 peel the nebulous veil off two tragic prophecies that will forever stand as Nostradamus' first successes foretelling events from our new millennium. New York city is near latitude 45 degrees. It did not exist in Nostradamus' time, and his use of *nouveau* often points to prophecies about a great and 'new' Western nation of the future (also called 'Americh' in his prophecies), that will include great new cities grasping at tomorrow's skies with towers he called 'hollow mountains'. New York's correct latitude is between 40 and 41 degrees. One might say Nostradamus got his calculations wrong, unless he foresaw in his vision the great and smoking wound left in the North Tower of the World Trade Center by the impact of the hijacked Boeing 767 passenger jet. Look for yourself at those unforgettable first pictures. The angle of the jet's mortal thrust was at 45 degrees!

Lines 2 and 3 describe the flaming engines of both commandeered jet airliners approaching the great new city. They crash into the World Trade Center towers, sending fireballs of *scattered flame* larger than the entire town in which Nostradamus wrote this prophecy 445 years before.

The last line is the key. You will know a future terrorist attack on New York City has come, when the victims are asking the French to verify that an attack is at hand. There are a number of reports coming from credible news sources, such as the Associated Press and

At forty-five degrees latitude, the sky will burn,
Fire approaches the great new city,
Immediately a huge, scattered flame leaps up...
(6 Q97)

the French newspaper, *Le Figaro*, that prove without a doubt that on 10 September French intelligence sources did warn their American opposites that al-Qaeda terrorists were on the move and American assets in Europe and the United States were threatened by immediate attack. The following morning saw American intelligence officers in Washington D.C. violently interrupted from their feverish efforts to verify the French claims by one of four airliners hijacked by al-Qaeda terrorists crashing into the Pentagon. Finally, even the quatrain indexing hides what could be a dating. As we will see later, the attack of the man who Nostradamus calls 'the Third Antichrist' comes shortly after the passing of a great comet. The quatrain's indexing of '97' may stand for the passing of Comet Hale-Bopp in 1997.

A second prophecy narrows the focus on New York as Nostradamus' intended 'new city' under attack:

> *Iardin du monde aupres du cité neufue,*
> *Dans le chemin des montaignes cauees:*
> *Sera faifi & plongé dans la Cuue,*
> *Beuuant par force eaux foulfre enuenimees.*

Garden of the world near the new city,
In the path of the hollow mountains:
It will be seized and plunged into a boiling cauldron,
Drinking by force the waters poisoned by sulphur.

(Century 10 : Quatrain 49)

117

If you were to stand on the western shore of the Hudson River, in New Jersey (also known as the 'Garden State'), and look across to Manhattan Island, you would see the man-made 'mountains' of the 'world' Trade Center in New York City. Imagine a 16th-century man's awe when he beholds two towers with 110 acre-sized storeys apiece climbing ten times higher than the highest cathedrals of his day. Would you not call such impossible monoliths, with 50,000 workers teeming inside, *hollow mountains*? Even New Yorkers describe their boulevards among the angular stone and steel crags of their skyscrapers as 'canyons'. If you wished to reach these twin Everests by rapid transit, it seems the prophet himself has directed you to use the 'Path' subway. He calls it as much, using the French equivalent *chemin*. In fact, the second hijacked jet roared across the *Garden* State, casting its shadow over the waters of the Hudson that cover the very same 'Path' subway *in the path of the hollow mountains*.

After being stabbed from the air, the hollow mountains are 'seized and plunged' into the boiling 'vat', or *cuue* as Nostradamus describes it in Renaissance French. Previous translations have relied on the secondary meaning of *cuue* as a 'tub' or 'tank'. Perhaps Nostradamus, ever the word player, intended more than one of the word's meanings. It must be remembered that before construction crews erected the great towers of the World Trade Center they placed their six subterranean floors into a watertight floor and rectangular sea wall so that the waters of the Hudson River would never penetrate the complex and flood Manhattan's underground subway system. The architects and construction workers affectionately called this watertight foundation 'the tub'.

The primary definition of *cuue* is a fermenting cauldron; wherein, Nostradamus, a physician and cosmetics manufacturer by profession, would plunge materials for the mixing of his medicines and cosmetics. The cauldron would summon boiling clouds as objects were seized and thrown into it. The use of *cuue* is a poetic attempt to capture the vision of the vast and mortally wounded World Trade towers plunging to earth from their own weight, into the ferment of boiling clouds made of their own pulverized debris. The last line may describe the toxicity of the debris cloud that blanketed New York City, with the stench of numerous toxic materials including ample levels of asbestos dust.

The final line may also portray a future avoided. If the collapse of the towers had undermined the 'tub', the Hudson would have poured into the New York subway system. New York port and civic authorities were initially alarmed that the walls might have been compromised and sent teams into the ruined Path subway tunnel at the approaches of the devastation to check for signs of water. None fortunately was found; otherwise, the terrorist attack on *the great new city* of

New York might have added thousands of unsuspecting victims, waiting along the subway stations or standing and sitting in their trundling compartments soaring through dark tunnels on their way to work. They would have suddenly found themselves forced to drink a wave of poisoned floodwaters, laced, as it were, with the *sulphur* of toxic debris from the World Trade Center towers.

This final line of Century 10 *Quatrain* 49 could also augur a future and far more catastrophic attack on New York. I sent my first warnings to my readers about the prophecy of an attack on New York's financial district as far back as 1983. Later, in 1995, my interpretation was dramatized on national US television for a Fox Network documentary entitled *Prophecies of the Millennium.*

While quoting the two prophecies above, the documentary pictured the World Trade Center vanishing in a fireball after which a mushroom cloud looms from the crater that was once the southern 'hollow mountain' range of Manhattan Island. I pray that the line *drinking by force the waters poisoned by sulphur* is a failed prophecy of what could be, rather than the next catastrophe waiting to be. Let us hope that the poisoned and sulphuric waters will never come from the detonation of an atomic device in the bilges of an unsuspected cargo ship in New York harbour. If New Yorkers are vigilant, this catastrophe will not occur.

The potential of such an event is implied elsewhere by a respected seer of the last century. America's Edgar

Cayce once described a waking dream where he was taken forward to the year 2100. Apparently, two bald and bespectacled scientists of that day, possessing unusually long beards, had 'discovered' Cayce in his future reincarnation. They took him on a tour over America in an anti-gravity, cigar-shaped flying machine. The world had suffered some vast natural disaster a century or so before. Some shift in the continents had made Nebraska – the place from which the ZZ-top scientists of the future plucked Cayce – into West Coast beachfront property. Later the trio flew over what remained of the ruins of New York, which at the time was undergoing the first stages of a reconstruction. Cayce could not tell whether New York had been destroyed by a natural calamity or by an attack.

In other readings held in a trance state Cayce had predicted a shift of the Earth's axis for some time shortly after 1998. It has not happened. Nebraska remains a haven for grain harvesters and not beachcombers. As of this writing (April 2002), the hollow mountains of New York, except for its beloved World Trade Towers, stand defiant against the prophecy of Cayce and my alternative interpretation for Nostradamus' vision. May they remain.

THE THIRD ANTICHRIST AND HIS 27-YEAR WAR

✳

At the time of this writing, no one has yet positively identified Nostradamus' Third Antichrist. In contrast to his certainty about Napoleon and Hitler (who he calls *Napaulon Roy* – Napoleon King – and *Hister*), Nostradamus is less clear who *Mabus*, the third tyrant, is. Perhaps this is an example of his prophetic myopia that enabled him to be clearest about events of local or European history. The prophet's vision tends to be cloudier when it contemplates future events in more distant lands. What does come through clearly is that this third and final Antichrist is not a prominent European leader. He may even be some obscure future terrorist who will trigger World War III with a weapon of mass destruction if we do not identify and restrain him in time.

> *Vn qui les dieux d'Annibal infernaux,*
> *Fera renaiſtre, effrayeur des humains:*
> *Oncq' plus d'horreur ne plus dire iournaulx,*
> *Qu'auint viendra par Babel aux Romains.*

One who the infernal gods of Hannibal [*Thurbo Majus*],
Will cause to be born, terror to all mankind:
Never more horror nor the newspapers tell of worse in the past,
Then will come to the Italians through Babel.

(Century 2 : Quatrain 30)

Mabus puis toft alors mourra, viendra,
De gens & beftes vne horrible defaite:
Puis tout à coup la vengeance on verra,
Cent, main, foif, faim, quand courra la comete.

Mabus [*Majus*] will soon die, then will come,
A horrible undoing of people and animals,
At once one will see vengeance,
One hundred powers, thirst, famine,
when the comet will pass.

(Century 2 : Quatrain 62)

L'antechrift trois bien toft annichiliez,
Vingt & fept ans fang durera fa guerre:
Les heretiques morts, captifs exilez,
Sang corps humain eau rogie grefler terre.

The Third Antichrist very soon annihilated,
Twenty-seven years his bloody war will last.
The heretics [*are*] dead, captives exiled,
Blood-soaked human bodies, and a reddened,
icy hail covering the earth.

(Century 8 : Quatrain 77)

These are the three prophecies in which one can find Nostradamus' third, and last, Antichrist. The first quatrain gives clues to his base of operations, his nationality and the place in Europe most vulnerable to his attack. The second quatrain gives us leads to decode his name, describe his act of horror and record the vengeance of the devastating counterstroke – all to take place on, or shortly after, the significant transit of a great comet across our skies. The third prophecy parallels themes in the second then expands on just what Mabus the Third Antichrist's *horrible undoing of people and animals* will be like.

Nostradamus hides the locale of his candidate Antichrist number three in the name of the *gods* honoured by Punic and Phoenician peoples, such as Hannibal. They were 'Baal' worshippers. Each region gave their Baal (Lord) God a personalized name. The Carthaginians called theirs 'Baal Hammon'. Nostradamus, the Christianized Jew, may be putting into play a pun of 'Hammon' and the derisive 'Mammon' to indicate his pro-Judeo-Christian bias against the final Antichrist. In addition, if you look at a modern map of regions marking the extent of Baal worship, you will see that it covers an area that today includes Tunisia, Libya, Palestine, Lebanon, Israel, Iraq and Syria.

The Romans had a custom of adopting the patron gods of a conquered nation and renaming them in Latin. After the Romans had sacked the city of Carthage at the close of the Third Punic War in 146 B.C., they built their own city over its ashes and renamed it Thurbo Majus. The enigmatic name M-A-B-U-S may stand as a classic anagram for 'M-A-J-U-S'.

What do the present-day ruins of an ancient city of Romanized, Baal Hammon worshippers have to do with the Third Antichrist? For one thing, it may indicate the importance of modern-day Tunisia as a base of operations for someone who would later earn the mantle *effrayeur* (terror) to all mankind. The ruins of Carthage are a few miles away from what once had been the chief headquarters and training camp for the PLO (the Palestine Liberation Organization). In its heyday during the seventies and early eighties, many figures who have been regarded (and may later be regarded) as radicals in the Palestinian freedom movement learned their infernal trade of terrorism just next door to the ruins of Thurbo Majus. Many of these men continue their quest in the new millennium to destroy Israel and establish a Palestinian state over its ashes from new bases in places once under the spiritual dominion of the Baal Gods of Hannibal: Lebanon, the West Bank, Jordan, Syria and Iraq (*Babel*).

The idea of newspapers was unknown in the time of Nostradamus. This fact makes it clear to anyone reading today's newspaper stories about Saddam Hussein, Abu Amar (better known as Yasser Arafat) Abu Nidal or Muammar Qaddafi, or the bombing of the New York Trade Center, that these clues have contemporary relevance. It also strongly implies that:

1. The next Antichrist after Napoleon and Hitler is from, or based in, North Africa or the Near East.

2. His weapon is terrorism.

3. The final line of 2 Q30 implies a horrendous and yet-unseen act of infamy coming either directly from, or supported by, *Babel* (modern-day Iraq). A number of extreme PLO factions have their offices in Baghdad, in Saddam Hussein's Iraq. The chief target in Europe will be Italy.

From 'Majus' we link to the *Mabus* prophecy of 2 Q62. Its themes parallel those from 8 Q77 to such an extent that I believe *the Third Antichrist* and Mabus can only be the same person. Both prophecies promise the rapid destruction of the Third Antichrist at the onset of his war. For instance, the first prediction says, *Mabus will soon die...* The second prediction slightly alters the phrase, saying the Third Antichrist is *very soon annihilated*. Once he dies, the first prophecy adds, *Then will come a horrible undoing of people and animals.* The second continues the same apocalyptic vision but becomes gruesomely specific about the dead and the dying. They are soaked and stained red by icy hail showers covering the entire earth.

Nostradamus' open-ended use of *terre* (earth) could have either a local or global use. Is this a description of some climatic catastrophe coming from a detonation of nuclear weapons? If so, then *a reddened, icy hail covering the earth* is a watered-down version of a nuclear winter – or better – nuclear autumn. Dust from atomic fire clouds could cool down the climate after a sustained nuclear attack on those countries deemed part of American President Bush's Marvel-comic moniker, the Axis of Evil. States such as Iraq, Iran and Syria who harbour terrorists in the Near East or states such as North Korea, who create and export the means to manufacture mass destruction, might suffer a retaliatory nuclear attack.

Is there another interpretation?

Nostradamus is a man of the Renaissance period. He could find it hard to explain a future plague raining from biological and chemical agents. A *terrible undoing of people and animals* hints at a weapon that unleashes poisons or plagues that can extinguish both animals and humans. To him the scene of *blood-soaked human bodies* under a *reddened, icy hail* may be his attempt to understand and communicate a vision of a chemical or biological attack. There are photographs from the late 1980s of Kurdish victims piled in the streets of their village after Saddam Hussein's Iraqi forces detonated chemical weapons over their heads. Witnesses said the weapons unleashed clouds of reddish and milky agents,

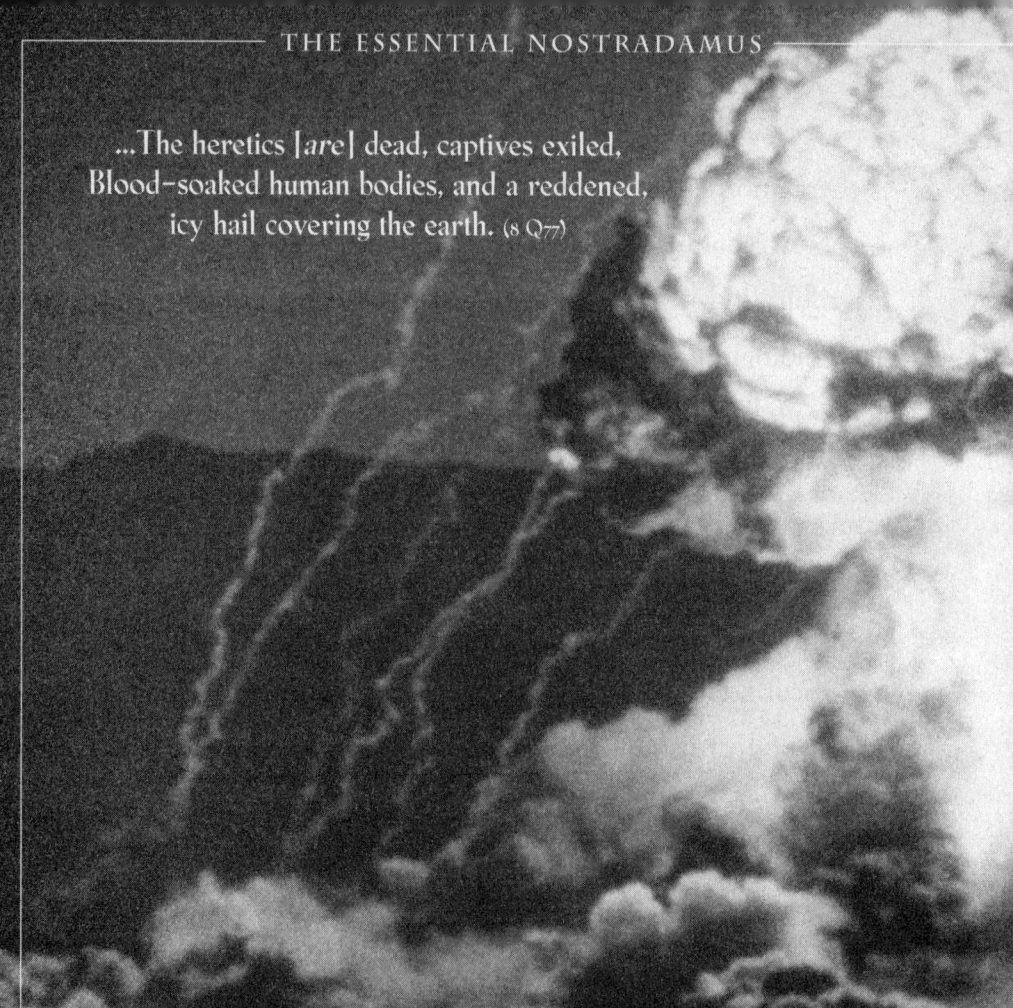

...The heretics [*are*] dead, captives exiled,
Blood-soaked human bodies, and a reddened,
icy hail covering the earth. (8 Q77)

staining their human and animal victims with red and white milky droplets. Thus, a milky rain in our future that kills both human beings and animals alike can come from a metaphorical hail shower of chemical or biological vapours; or, fall from the sky in a reddish black rain laced with radioactive fallout such as that seen at Hiroshima.

The closing words of the Mabus prophecy of Century 2 Quatrain 62 imply an overwhelming counterattack: *At once one will see vengeance* coming from *one hundred powers.* The US coalition formed after 11 September 2001 against a perceived global terrorist network numbers around one hundred nations.

Mentions of *thirst* and *famine* are common in what

one could call Nostradamus' numerous Third World War prophecies. You will know such a war is near when there is a global plague of droughts and famines. They exist today, and they are growing from the continued stress placed on the food, water and eco-systems from an unrepentant and inexorable overabundance of more people demanding their share of less. The prophecy describing what could be the 'Pearl Harbor' surprise attack that brings America into World War III is indexed quatrain number 97 in Century 6 of Nostradamus' prophecies. That would make 1997 the date for a cosmic omen forewarning us that the advent of Mabus, the famine, the thirst and war was soon to come. That stellar emissary was none other than the great bearded star, Hale-Bopp.

The 'Third Antichrist' prophecy of Century 8 Quatrain 77 could label the shadowy minions of Mabus as *heretics*. Are these the secular renegade operatives of the PLO, like Yasser Arafat, who turned away in youth from their religion? Are they other terrorists who submit to a religiously extreme and apocalyptic aberration of Islam? Whatever the case, the prophecy points to their eventual capture, exile and death. One may already see the first of these Near Eastern exiles sitting blindfolded in their red jail jumpsuits at Camp X-ray – the US concentration camp established at Guantanamo Bay, Cuba.

Who, then, is a candidate for Mabus?

I have followed the etymological trail for decades, trying to uncover clues to just what Nostradamus meant by the name. I still believe that the weight of his interests and prejudices pull the divining rod of possibility towards the magnetic hotbed of Middle Eastern and North Africa despots. Today's Arab and Iranian terrorists and misguided zealots are our prime suspects. For me the Mabus mug shot is flashed upon the film of my curiosity by Nostradamus' favoured mind-melding 'camera' of classical metaphors. In other words, I have seen him too often colour his prophecies in the Kodak moment of Ancient Greek and Roman images of the future. If the Ancient Romans called the Danube 'Hister', Nostradamus would hide his Second Antichrist's name behind that classical Roman label. He would cloak a vision of a child dreaming his diabolical dreams while resting on the banks of the 'Hister' and hide the name of the young Adolf 'Hitler'.

A study of the last two antichrists indicates that most of the letters needed to decode the name of the Third Antichrist could be found in his enigmatic name. For instance: PAU NAY OLORON (in Century 8 Quatrain 1) becomes Napaulon Roy (Napoleon King); Hister easily becomes Adolf 'Hitler'. In this way, if Nostradamus is being consistent then we should find the name of the next and final antichrist virtually hiding in the letters M-A-B-U-S.

Certainly, at the time of this writing in April of

2002, the next terrorist leader caught in US sights can be found by reversing the letters 'mabus' to 'subam' then reverse any letters again, such as a 'b' into a 'd' to get 'sudam'. That leaves one the freedom in anagramming to replace one vowel 'u' with an 'a' to get 'Sadam'. The law of eliminating or adding redundancies to letters allows one to double our 'd' to get 'Saddam' Hussein.

Play the same game with the founder of the al-Qaeda terrorist organization, Usama bin Laden, and you can find that u-s-a-m-a + b has nearly all the fixings to cook Nostradamus' code name: 'Maaus + b'. You need not take the 'b' from 'bin' Laden to replace one redundant 'a', but if you wish you can take the 'b' and get 'Maabus' then cut the redundant 'a' to get 'Mabus'.

After the events of September 11, 2002, I have received what I might call 'new leads' from hundreds of my readers. Many of the leads are products of ignorance and naïvety, but some of you are members of my HogueProphecy mailing list and are onto something deserving a commentary.

There are many out there who believe that only the country with the preeminent arsenal of weapons of mass destruction (the United States to be exact) could cause 'a horrible undoing of people and animals' coming from their counterattack on those who might cause their leader to fall early in the conflict. To these interpreters of Nostradamus, US President G. W. Bush is their 'Mabus'.

Does the idea wash? Maybe. The laws of anagram will allow one to rotate letters 180 degrees in lower case. Roll the letters 'm, a' of 'Mabus' on their heads and you get 'gw'. The 'h' in Latin is silent, thus the result is 'gw Bus(h)' for (G)eorge (W)alker Bush.

Personally, I do not subscribe to this theory. People leaning politically to the left will argue with some efficacy that President Bush's unilateral and often dictatorial foreign policies – painting over the grey and complex issues with often simplistic, black and white 'them or us' brushstrokes – might contribute to a climate of global terrorism, but that does not mean he is the man Nostradamus tagged as 'Mabus'. Still, for the record I cannot rule out that I may be in error in my view that

Mabus and the Third Antichrist are one person. It is possible that 2 Q62 and 8 Q77 are describing Mabus and the Third Antichrist as two figures pitted at war with each other. However, if this is in fact Nostradamus' intent, then both combatants will be early casualties in their war of wills.

Certainly, even a prophet can mistake two leaders who are bound together by a shared dark destiny as one antichrist, when viewing a far-off future. Perhaps he has mistaken them for two sides of the same coin of evil. The court of future history and events will be the final judge.

If the interpretations presented here are correct then the criterion the future will use to reach that judgment depends on the fulfilment of the following events:

1. Whoever Mabus is, he is one of the first to fall in the war he launches, be it a war on America or a war on terrorism.

2. His death will create a war cry for revenge and there will be a devastating counterattack.

3. The reaction to his martyrdom and the counterattack will set in motion a 27-year war that first sees terrorism as its opening stage but could eventually escalate and widen its theatre of destruction to include an exchange of nuclear, biological and chemical weapons between a number of nations. This may include the worst-case scenario of a potential three-way war fought between the

United States, Russia and China over food and other resources in the 2020s. In other words, a World War III of terrorism becomes a world war 'free' for all.

I believe the fulfilment of the first step is likely to happen before the end of 2002, and will certainly happen before 2004. Now let us play the three-step scenario with each of our top candidates for Mabus:

USAMA BIN LADEN

Usama bin Laden = maaus b(in Laden) = maabus = Mabus?

It seems Usama bin Laden may have already died. Not from the extreme prejudice of US smart bombs breathing fireballs over him in an Afghani cave, but from want of finding a working dialysis machine in a devastated, Third-World-medieval country. If his body is not recovered then there are those in the Islamic world who might wrap the apocalyptic myth of the Twelfth Imam around his buried shoulders. He will be their champion, hiding in some secret place, until he rises again to lead the Islamic world to Allah's final victory against their satanic Christian and Jewish enemies. Until that fictional day arrives, (Maabus) bin Laden's name will be the war cry for another 27 years of terrorist attacks.

YASSER ARAFAT

Yasser Arafat (PLO code name: Abu Amar) = maaabur =
mabu(s) = Mabus? Or: Abu = (M)abu(s) = Mabus?

Yasser Arafat may soon die a martyr. Easter 2002 has seen the beginning of his planned last stand against the Israelis, code named 'The Field of Thorns'. The Palestinians will dupe the Israeli Army into reoccupying the West Bank to fight an urban guerilla war. Arafat and his leadership hope the massacre of hundreds of Palestinian civilians will cause a global outcry against the Israeli occupation, thus bringing international peacekeepers and ultimately a political solution more in tune with Arafat's designs. In the worst-case scenario, Arafat becomes a martyr and the Arab world rises up in a region-wide war against Israel and its

American ally. Such a consequence arising from Arafat's early martyrdom would point strongly to him as Nostradamus' intended Mabus.

SADDAM HUSSEIN
Saddam Hussein = maddas = sadam = subam = Mabus

If Mabus is not Yasser Arafat, then another Arab martyr could come from the actions of the United States moving blindly forward with their plans to invade Iraq to overthrow Saddam Hussein. I have stated since 1997 that Nostradamus' quatrains imply that Saddam would face death from a cruise missile cutting into the bowels of one of his reinforced bunkers. (See pp.740–41 of *Nostradamus: The Complete Prophecies*.) Thus he, as the Mabus prophecy says, 'soon dies'. The rapid overthrow and extermination of Saddam makes him Mabus if a 'horrible undoing of people and animals' follows the disintegration of Iraq as a country. The collapse of post-

Saddam Iraq could destabilize the Middle East as it draws another president from Texas into his own version of a Vietnam quagmire.

GEORGE W. BUSH
G. W. Bush = g.w. Bus(h) = M. a. Bus = Mabus?

Now, for Mabus to be the American president, 'gw Bus(h)', he must be one of the first to fall in his war against (or 'of') terrorism. It must be noted that the American president has often made forceful, albeit linguistically simplistic and repetitive, attempts to remind the American people that his war on terror could last as long as two to three decades. In other words up to or beyond the 27 years predicted by Nostradamus. If he were to be killed and it was proven that his death came at the hands of terrorists, then we could certainly see the 'horrible undoing of people and animals' coming from an all-out American revenge attack on those nations of the

East that are viewed by the Bush administration as bases for international terrorist groups.

The rhetoric has already escalated. January 2002 closed with President Bush giving his first State of the Union speech before Congress – now immortalized as the 'Axis of Evil' speech. In it, the president defined any nation that harbours terrorists and seeks weapons of mass destruction as 'evil'. In other words, President Bush has officially added Iran and North Korea to his target list with Saddam Hussein's Iraq. The leader of the free world – who has at his disposal the largest arsenal of nuclear, biological and chemical weapons in history – has condemned these countries as 'evil' for trying to procure their own. Henceforth, he has put them on notice that at any time they may face the full economic and military wrath of the United States unless they curtail any association with terrorist organizations, and stop seeking, exporting or manufacturing weapons of mass destruction.

After making his State of the Union ultimatum, the president closed January with each new version of his 'Axis of Evil' speech breathing yet more fire and brimstone bellicosity. In turn, the leaders of Iraq and Iran have dismissed Bush's new Marvel-comics-like label with their own sweeping and categorically cartoon-literate reactions. Saddam Hussein called Bush's Axis of Evil definition 'stupid'. President Khatami of Iran first publicly stated his 'sadness' at the US president's aggressive and sweeping definition of Iran as an 'evil' nation. Iran's supreme religious leader and *de facto* ruler, Ayatollah Ali Khamenei, called Bush 'a big-mouth'. The official response from the North Korean government described Bush's statement as tantamount to a declaration of war and then concluded rather ominously, 'A first strike capability is not the exclusive option of the United States.' Adding insult to brinkmanship, many US television news channels offered up images of Kim Dae Jung, the democratically elected president of South Korea, when commenting on North Korea and its dictator, Kim Jong Il.

Bush's Axis of Evil label and his ever more strident 'you are either with us or against us' stance have already hurt the popular movement of moderates inside Iran. Rather than strengthen the quiet revolution to overthrow Islamic extremism in the Iranian government, Bush's definition is generally viewed by Iranians as a condemnation of their whole nation. A renewed fear of a US attack has only strengthened the power of the committee of Ayatollahs who are a law above the religiously moderate President Khatami.

Europeans and their leaders view Bush's free and ever more frequent use of the 'E' word (evil) with ever-greater foreboding. The United States' closest Western European allies voice their unease at what appears to be his intention to dictate terms and strategies unilaterally. Yet, President Bush's new level of rousing rhetoric saw his popularity in some American polls rise beyond the 80 percent mark in the month following his Axis of Evil declaration.

Although many people, mostly outside the US, view Bush's combativeness and unilateralism as becoming as much a part of the problem as those nations harbouring terrorists, his critics should take notice that the president and his handlers may be onto something.

I believe George W. Bush has correctly defined the new axis alliance of a new world war, and Nostradamus may have foreseen it centuries before one of Bush's speech-writers wrote the phrase 'Axis of Evil' for him only to be mysteriously dismissed from the White House Staff shortly afterwards.

The Axis of Evil vs. The 'Brothers of the North'

❋

For 15 years and counting, I have published my belief that a passage from Nostradamus' *Epistle to King Henry II of France*, written in 1558, defined the alliances and bloody outcome of a future war waged between two great northern superpowers and an Eastern 'triumvirate' of terrorist nations. I present the following passage from the *Epistle* and my translation and interpretation, taken from pages 588–91 of *Nostradamus: The Complete Prophecies.* It is the most comprehensive synthesis of all the elements of a number of recorded interpretations I have made through the years about the triumvirate-of-terror (Axis of Evil) theme. In fact, most of the following interpretations, which were published in 1997, found themselves in articles printed as far back as 1984.

Quelle grande oppression que par lors sera faicte
sus les princes & gouuerneurs des royaumes,
mesmes de ceux qui seront maritimes & orientaux
& leurs langues entremeslees à grande societe,
la langue des Latins & des Arabes par la

cõmunication punique, & seront tous ces Roys
orientaux chassez, profligez, exterminez,
non du tout par le moyen des forces des Roys
d'Aquilon, & par la proximité de nostre siecle par le
moyen des trois vnys secretrement cerchãt la mort
& insidies par embusches l'vn de l'autre, & durera
le renouuellement de triumuirat sept ans, que la
renommee de telle secte fera son estendue par
l'vniuers & sera soubstenu le sacrifice de la saincte
& immaculee hostie, & seront lors les Seigneurs
deux en nombre d'Aquilon victorieux sur les
orientaux, & sera en iceux faict si grand bruict
& tumulte bellique, que tout iceluy orient tremblera
de l'effrayeur d'iceux freres non freres Aquilonaires.

What a great oppression then will fall upon the princes and governors of kingdoms and especially those that shall live near the sea and eastward, their language intermixed [in a great society of nations]; the language of the Latin nations and of the Arabic intermixed via the North African interchange, and all these Eastern Kings shall be driven away, beaten and annihilated, not altogether by the means of the forces from the Kings of the North — and by the near proximity of our century — by means of three secretly united seeking for death by ambushes [terrorism] one against the other; and the renewal of the Triumvirate shall last for seven years; yet, the fame of such a sect shall spread the world over, and the sacrifice of the holy and immaculate host shall be upheld, and then shall the lords be two in number of the North [bloc?], victorious over the Eastern ones, and there shall be a great noise and warlike tumult that all the East shall quake and fear those two brothers of the North who are yet not brothers.

'Nostradamus steps back to paint us a broader picture of what appears to be World War III alliances. Sides will be drawn seven years before the end of the 20th century, or the war will be fought some time after 1999 and will last for seven years. A triumvirate of *Eastern Kings* will secretly unite, using ambushes and anarchy as their main weapons against their chief nemeses, the *Kings of the North* – possibly America, the EC and Russia. Language *intermixed in a great society of nations* places this prophecy in modern times. Note the *North African* allusion to Tunisia, the headquarters of the PLO. Libya's close ties with France and Italy through oil are also implied. Because Nostradamus usually defines all points beyond Greece as Asia, this Eastern alliance has every chance of being a *Mid-Eastern* and even North African Axis alliance.

'I can only assume from continual references throughout the Bible, and the auguring of Nostradamus and other prophetic giants such as Edgar Cayce and Cheiro (Count Louis Hamon), that the three most likely combinations for candidates for this triumvirate are Libya, Syria and Iran; Egypt, Syria and Iran; or even Sudan, Libya and Iran. Elsewhere in the quatrains, we have already examined references to *Mesopotamia* – Iraq – playing a primary role in the greater war to come. Operation Desert Storm may be no more than an early episode in a long pan-Islamic war with the West that will make some of America's staunchest Arab Coalition allies, like Syria and Egypt, into greater enemies than the Iraqis. Whoever the Mid-Eastern *triumvirate* finally turns out to be, they will find support from some greater *Eastern King*, implying the leader of the People's Republic of China or North Korea.

'The Arab triumvirate and its Eastern ally, China,

suffer the mother of all massacres through the overwhelming firepower of the great northern powers. If by *near proximity of our century*, Nostradamus means Armageddon is at hand, he is as inaccurate on dating the final battle as St John of Revelation was in the first century A.D., when he slotted the Second Coming of Christ in his own near future.

'Nostradamus, like many of history's greatest prophets, shares a collective vision that the Cold War scenario had little prophetic weight. If there is to be a Third World War, it will come from a conflict of biblical proportions in the Middle East. Moreover, the quatrains strongly suggest that such a war comes only *after* Russia drops communism and is *brothers*, or friends, with the

United States. Reader beware, the brotherhood is premature. When Nostradamus says they *are yet not brothers*, he makes a word-play link to 2 Q89's two great *friends* who are *halved*. Nostradamus uses *demis*, which can be the French *d'amis* (of friends), or the Latin word *demis* (being 'halved' or 'split' apart). The instigator for this split could be *Mabus* (2 Q62) and/or the Third Antichrist, who may use submarines based in either Libya or the Persian Gulf to trigger a terrorist event so horrendous that it undermines the Russo-American alliance.'

THE MAN FROM THE EAST

✳

Tant attendu ne reuiendra iamais,
Dedans l'Europe, en Afie apparoiftra:
Vn de la ligue yflu du grand Hermes,
Et fur tous Roys des orients croiftra.

Long awaited he will never return.
He will appear in Asia [*and be*] at home in Europe:
One who is issued from great Hermes,
And over all the Kings of the East will he grow.

(Century 10 : Quatrain 75)

Nostradamus has made it clear that the next great spiritual master is coming from the East. He had to cloak his revelation so as not to be burned as a heretic. But if one can perceive the hidden message between the lines of dozens of prophecies, it is clear that he is warning us not to look for the second coming of some gentile made-over blond and blue-eyed Hollywood Jesus, nor should we expect some dark-haired and kosher man from Galilee named Y'shua.

The *Long awaited* projection of Jesus Christ we have created *will never return.*

The new world teacher will be from India or the Far East. He will issue from the non-dualistic teachings of Hermes. The Hermetic message is very close to the

Eastern Tantric path, which teaches, 'As above, so below; all is divine.' In the Hermetic and Tantric paths, there is no Hell to fear or Heaven to pine for. These are childish illusions. No God exists outside of you. Without your awakened eyes and heart, God cannot perceive or love his universe. Without your understanding transcending judgments and conditioning, there is no transcendental state of God. Without your enlightenment, God is as fast asleep as you are. In short, the Hermetic and Tantra visions propose that your existence is either a paradise or a hell of your making, and no saviour will be coming to carry your burdens. The Aquarian Age is about impersonal messianic phenomena – no sheep, no shepherds, no bleeding messiahs. The masters of the future may point the way, but it is your life to live and your universe to travel.

Nostradamus describes this world teacher to be in the manner of Hermes, who was also worshipped as a God of Thieves. This new 'Jesus' is a very different 'thief in the night' than the one expected by mainstream religions.

Whether the many gurus and god men bringing the spiritual values of the East to the Western world for over a century and counting are charlatans or true shamans of a new religiousness is still unknown. What is certain is that seeds of a century of Eastern teachers have been planted in Western hearts and minds. We await their full flowering in the 21st century.

The quatrain's indexing may give us a hint of a key

year for the advent to the West of Nostradamus' Man from the East: 'Q75' = 1975, the year Madame Blavatsky, the Russian seeress and founder of Theosophy, predicted the appearance of 'a messenger to come to the west in 1975'.

> *Celuy qu'aura la charge de destruire*
> *Temples, & sectes, changez par fantasie:*
> *Plus aux rochiers qu'aux viuans viendra nuire,*
> *Par langue ornee d'oreilles reffasie.*

A man who will be charged with destroying
Temples and sects altered by fantasy:
He will harm the rocks rather than the living,
Ears filled with ornate speeches.

(Century 1 : Quatrain 96)

The idea that traditional religions are a fantasy or a shadow of their original living teaching is a recurring theme for Nostradamus. The man mentioned here must be a pioneering mystic who will strike out against old rock-like dogmas, earning the unified wrath of the world's organized religions. We will know him as an eloquent and compelling speaker. The Indian mystic Osho was put in chains in America in 1985. Unification Church leader Sun Myung Moon was vilified. He was first imprisoned by the North Koreans and later served a term in prison in America. Bahá'í mystic 'Abdu'l-Bahá and his father before him (Bahá'u'lláh) spent much of their lives in exile or in prison for their beliefs and teachings.

The year 1996 marks the beginning of a century-long decline of orthodox religions if the quatrain's indexing is a hidden date. By the year 2096 they will have completely faded away or changed beyond recognition.

NOSTRADAMUS' EIGHT CLUES TO THE FOUNDER OF THE COMING SPIRITUAL REVOLUTION

A number of Nostradamus' prophecies seem to chronicle the lives and actions of spiritual teachers and their movements from no later than the latter half of the 20th century. The pattern of these prophecies indicates the unique historical phenomenon we call the Human Potential or New Age movement.

Within this movement are many groups (both fraudulent and genuine) that experiment with alternative lifestyles, philosophies and religions, often Eastern in origin, and practise new psychological and physical therapies. These groups, although not always in agreement over details, are mostly concerned with discovering new paths to world peace and ecological balance. All strive to awaken humankind to its potential for higher consciousness.

These prophecies can be gathered into eight specific categories. They are the prophet's eight clues to the character of the coming new religion, its non-dogmatic and individualistic teachings, and to the identification of its visionaries.

The eight clues and their corresponding quatrains are:

Clue 1. A Man from the East will be at Home in the West. A great spiritual catalyst from Asia finds his teachings welcomed in the West, primarily in Europe and America. Nostradamus maps out his flight to Europe via crossing the Apennine Mountains of Italy to first see France.

> *Dedans l'Europe, en Afie apparoiftra...* (10 Q75)

> *L'Oriental fortira de fon fiege, paffer*
> *les monts Apennins voir la Gaule:*
> *Tranfpercera le ciel...* (2 Q29)

> **He will appear in Asia [*and be*]**
> **at home in Europe...** (10 Q75)

The man from the East will come out of his seat,
passing across the Apennines to see France.
He will fly through the sky... (2 Q29)

Clue 2. The Rod of Hermes (after the caduceus wand of Hermes) indicates the teaching is non-dualistic.

Tranfpercera le ciel, les eaux & neige,
et vn chafcun frappera de fa gaule. (2 Q29)

Du pont Euxine, & la grand Tartarie, vn Roy fera qui
viendra voir la Gaule: tranfpercera Alane & l'Armenie,
et dans Bifance lairra fanglante Gaule. (5 Q54)

...Dedans l'Europe, en Afie apparoiftra:
Vn de la ligue yflu du grand Hermes... (10 Q75)

He will fly through the sky, the rains and the
snows and strike everyone with his rod. (2 Q29)

From the Black Sea, and great Tartary,
there will be a king who will come to see France:
[*he*] will penetrate through Russia and Armenia,
and into Byzantium [Istanbul],
he will leave his bloody rod. (5 Q54)

...He will appear in Asia, at home in Europe:
One who is issued from great Hermes... (10 Q75)

Clue 3. Outlawed Teacher. The status quo religions will
try to prevent this teacher from travelling freely around
the world. This rebel mystic will harm the 'rocks' of

religious dogma rather than the existential religious nature of the living who are metaphorically imprisoned inside of them. The eloquence of this traveller will crack open the dogma rock and awaken the seed of religiousness in the listener.

Celuy qu'aura la charge de destruire temples, & sectes,
changez par fantasie: plus aux rochiers qu'aux viuans
viendra nuire, par langue ornee d'oreilles reffasie. (1 Q96)

A man will be charged with destroying
temples and sects altered by fantasy:
He will harm the rocks rather than the living,
Ears filled with ornate speeches. (1 Q96)

Clue 4. Mystic Rose. The *rose* or *red* colours, along with all the red shades of sunset, symbolize the teachings from the East and are applied to the colours worn by disciples of the Eastern teachers. The 'middle' way, a Buddhist teaching, is also implied. It gains greater popularity in the West at a time when the plague of war increases, as during our own times. Know this mystic is among us when silence is his message – his truth. Know also that he will come late, as truth always does to a world that nourishes the egoist in all of us. The majority of us will recognize him after he is dead. The 'red ones' gathering around him are red-cloaked disciples that will live in controversy and persecution from the mainstream world. Know that the Man from the East, and his message of silence and peace, comes before advent of the Third Antichrist (prior to the passing of the Comet Hale-Bopp in 1997).

Sur le milieu du grand monde la rofe, pour nouueaux faicts fang public efpandu: a dire vray on aura bouche clofe, lors au befoing viendra tard l'attendu. (5 Q96)

Contre les rouges fectes fe banderont, feu, eau, fer, corde par paix fe minera, au point mourir, ceux qui machineront, fors vn que monde fur tout ruynera. (9 Q51)

Upon the middle of the great world – the rose. For new deeds public blood shed. To speak the truth they will have closed mouths. Then at the time of need the awaited one will come late. (5 Q96)

Against the red sects religions will conspire.
Fire, water, steel, the accord through peace to weaken.
On the point of dying, those who will contrive, except
one who above all the world will ruin. (9 Q51)

Clue 5. Mars and Flame. The new religious rebellion symbolized by a *red-as-revolution flame* is poised to burn down the dogmas of the past. Many prophets foresee a purification of humanity *by fire*. It is for us to choose whether this fire is one of global warming, a Third World War of international terrorism, or a fire of new religious self-awareness and consciousness. It will be a time when mainstream religions are racked with scandals and corruption. The people of that day will ask why they slavishly adopted into their lives what appear ever more clearly to be outmoded and even fossilized religious traditions.

...Et eſtant proche d'vne autre deſolation, par lors qu'elle fera à ſa plus haute & ſublime dignité... à ce que naiſtra d'vn rameau de la ſterille, de long temps, qui deliurera le peuple vniuers de celle ſeruitude benigne & volontaire ſoy remettant à la protection de Mars... de telle ſecte fera ſon eſtendue par l'vniuers... (Epistle to Henry II)

...At the eve of another desolation when the perverted church is atop her most high and sublime dignity... there will proceed one born from a branch long barren, who will deliver the people

of the world from a meek and voluntary slavery
and place them under the protection of Mars...
the flame of a sect shall spread the world over...

(Epistle to Henry II)

Clue 6. Diana, Dhyana, the *Moon* and Meditation. The
Science of Self-Observation is the fundamental tenet of
the next global religion. The Moon applies either to the
feminine and intuitive aspects of the new religion or to
the name of one or more of the spiritual catalysts.

Vous verrez toſt & tard faire grand change, horreurs
extremes & vindications: que ſi la lune conduicte par ſon
ange, le Ciel s'approche des inclinations. (1 Q56)

Le penultiefme du furnom du prophete,
prendra Diane pour fon iour & repos... (2 Q28)

Le tant d'argent de Diane & Mercur, les fimulacres
au lac feront trouuez: le figulier cherchant argille neufue,
luy & les fiens d'or feront abbreuez. (9 Q12)

La Lune au plain de nuict fur le haut mont, le nouueau
fophe d'vn feul cerueau l'a veu: par fes difciples eftre immortel femond,
yeux au midy, en feins mains, corps au feu. (4 Q31)

Sooner and later you will see great changes, extreme horrors
and vengeances. For the moon is led by its angel,
The heavens approach the Balance.
[*Astrological* **]** (1 Q56)

Second to the last of the prophet's name will take Diana's
day [the moon's day] as his day of silent rest... (2 Q28)

The great amount of silver of Diana [*moon*]
and Mercury [*Hermes*]. The images will be seen
in the lake [*a metaphor for the still mind in meditation*].
The sculptor looking for new clay. He and his followers
will be soaked in gold [*a Hermetic reference to the
attainment of enlightenment*]. (9 Q12)

The Moon in the middle of the night...
the young sage alone with his mind has seen it.
His disciples invite him to become immortal...
his body in the fire. (4 Q31)

Clue 7. The Infuriating Traveller. The more controversial the globetrotting spiritual catalyst is, the more likely he is a visionary Nostradamus intended. No spiritual teacher in history has been accepted by the mainstream religions while they are alive. They are called mind-controllers and cultists today just as Buddha, Mohammed and Jesus Christ were called when they walked the Earth.

Prendra Diane pour fon iour & repos: loing vaguera par frenetique tefte, et deliurant vn grand peuple d'impos. (2 Q28)

...[He] will take Diana's day as his day of silent rest. He will travel far and wide in his drive to infuriate, delivering a great people from subjection. (2 Q28)

Clue 8. Strange Birds crying 'Now!' The strange birds are the spiritual teacher and his disciples calling upon humanity to wake up now before it is too late.

...en apres l'antechrist fera le prince infernal, encores par la derniere foy... tous les Royaumes de la Chrestienté, & auffi des infideles, par l'efpace de vingt cinq ans, & feront plus grieues guerres & batailles, & feront villes, citez, chafteaux, & tous autres edifices bruflez, defolez... & tant de maux fe commettront par le moyen de Satan, prince infernal, que prefque le monde vniuerfel fe trouuera defaict & defolé: & auant iceux aduenements, aucuns oyfeaux infolites crieront par l'air. Huy, huy, & feront apres quelque temps efuanouys.

(Epistle to Henry II)

191

...The Antichrist returns for the last time...
all the Christian and infidel nations will
tremble for the space of twenty-five years
and wars and battles will be more grievous
than ever, and towns, cities, citadels and all
other structures will be destroyed... so
many evils by Satan's prince will be
committed that almost the entire world
will find itself undone and desolated:
Before these events many rare birds will
cry in the air. 'Now!' 'Now!' and
some time later will vanish.

(Epistle to Henry II)

THE 11 CANDIDATES FOR THE MAN FROM THE EAST

In this section we will consider 11 personalities in the light of the prophet's Eight Clues who plant the seed for a spiritual rebellion in the latter half of the 20th century, which will later bloom as a response to the travails about to overtake us in the 21st century. Nostradamus narrows the list to those either fitting within the parameters of coming from the East no later than just prior to 1997, or those Westerners prior to 1997 that drew most of their inspiration from Eastern, non-dualistic teachings. A third requirement is that the teacher will be a rebel, even in the eyes of his own Eastern religious roots. Even better, know that he is the one foreseen by Nostradamus if he upsets all sides on the religious debate while alive, yet leaves behind a vibrant and spreading movement of disciples.

SWAMI PARAMAHANSA YOGANANDA (1893–1952)
Indian Mystic, Founder of the Self-Realization Fellowship

Yogananda introduced Kriya Yoga to the West and taught that the mind and heart could be raised from a limited moral consciousness into union (yoga) with the consciousness of God. Yogananda and his disciples sometimes wore orange robes in the Eastern tradition of the seeker (see Clue 5). One can apply to Yogananda Nostradamus' references to a man from the East, colours of flame, teachings flowering in the West and intensive travel. Yogananda's desire to synthesize the beliefs of the established religions of the world make him unlikely to be the one against whom *religions will conspire* (see Clue 4). The new millennium has seen Yogananda and his followers rapidly distance themselves from any action or religious concept that one could deem as opposed by established religion and his movement has blended with all the ever more religiously correct movements of what is called the Mind-Body-Spirit, or New Age mainstream.

MEHER BABA (1894–1969)
Indian Sufi Mystic

Meher Baba, a Parsi, born in Poona, India, was a master of the devotional path of Sufism. He was opposed to religious hierarchy, ritual and ceremony, and his motto was, 'Don't worry, be happy.' His followers set up 'Baba Lover' centres all over the world and, in America alone, Baba's teaching attracted an estimated 6,000 disciples. He was indeed a rebel, but a peaceful one: his teachings were neither inflammatory nor designed to anger the established religions – he was no infuriating traveller (see Clue 7). Although his philosophy did include the concept of living in the *Now* (Clue 8), it contains no bird symbolism, no moon aspect – either symbolic or actual

– (see Clue 6), and no mention of either the colour red (see Clue 4), or of flames (see Clue 5). His movement has steadily declined since his passing in 1969.

SWAMI PRABHUPADA (1896–1978)
Founder of the Hare Krishna Movement

This Indian mystic initially came to the West during the late 1960s to spread the message of Krishna Consciousness among the flower children and hippie movements of that day, but later found a wider mainstream audience. In the East, the many shades of red in a flame are one of the symbols of consciousness. Prabhupada's singing and dancing Western followers wear the orange robes of ancient Krishna devotees.

Prabhupada's teachings, although new for people in the West, are based on ancient Hindu-Vedic scriptures, and he encourages his Western disciples to adopt the lifestyles prescribed by those traditional texts. Although the orange-robed Hare Krishnas have angered some and mostly puzzled many Westerners, it cannot be said that mainstream society views their existence as a dangerous threat to organized religious thinking. The movement has not significantly grown in size since the mid-1980s and seems to have passed its peak.

L. RON HUBBARD (1911–86)
Author of Dianetics ™,
Founder of the Church of Scientology

Scientology aims to help people recover spiritual health after suffering psychic and mental traumas, guiding them on the path towards reestablishing a 'clear' mental and spiritual state. The creator of Scientology, and his 'new' religion itself, have encountered opposition around the world and fought many legal and political battles. His Church has an estimated five million adherents and is considered dangerous by many established religions. One of its symbols is a flaming volcano (see Clue 5).

Hubbard drew most of his fundamental ideas for Scientology from Hinayana Buddhism and mainstream psychology. Thus his 'new' religion is a repackaging of a traditional Eastern and Buddhist dogma; or, *from the East* (see Clue 1) – even though he is not from the East himself. Hubbard was not born under *Mars* (see Clue 5), has no moon connection (see Clue 6) and does not follow a Hermetic tradition (see Clue 2). The Scientology movement does, however, enter the 21st century with a continued, yet slow, increase of adherents (and controversy), making it a new religion worth watching.

'ABDU'L-BAHÁ (1844–1921)
Leader of the Bahá'í faith

The eldest son and successor of Bahá'u'lláh, upon whose death he assumed full authority for the Bahá'í movement. He interpreted teachings that pave the way for a synthesis of all religions in a spiritual global village. Throughout much of his adult life, he spread the faith from his new religious seat on Mt. Carmel in Israel. Like his father, he had a prodigious correspondence with believers and inquirers around the globe, and endured long years of prison life. He made extensive tours to Europe and America and was a prophetic advocate for a League of Nations. Yet, despite the fact that the Bahá'í movement and its founding masters are Eastern (Iranian), and initially have provoked controversy in the West as the successful catalyst for the 20th century's new openness to interrelation of different faiths, the movement is not universally rejected as a cult by orthodox faiths, except by fundamentalist Islam. The new century sees millions of Bahá'ís continue their spread the world over, and although their message of peaceful rebellion through diplomacy has great merit, the movement does not conform to all of Nostradamus' eight clues.

G.I. GURDJIEFF (c.1877–49)
Master of The Fourth Way

Gurdjieff was born in Alexandropol in Russian Armenia. For some 20 years, his obsession with trying to understand life's strange and mysterious phenomena drove him to travel throughout the remotest regions of Tibet, Central Asia and the Middle East. Leaving Russia after the Bolshevik takeover, he established a communal spiritual campus outside Paris in 1922, and later set up a Gurdjieff school in America. His teachings are a revolutionary synthesis of Sufi, Central Asian and South Asian techniques of meditation and awareness training which he called 'The Fourth Way' – the other orthodox paths being the way of the yogi, the devotee and the sadhu. In 1924 he disbanded the Mystery School and devoted himself to recording his teachings in three volumes: *Beelzebub's Tales to His Grandson*, *Meetings with Remarkable Men* and finally *Life is real only then when 'I am'*. From 1933 onwards, he lived almost exclusively in Paris. His written teachings are a perennial fixture in the Mind-Body-Spirit genre. The new millennium sees Gurdjieff study groups continue to thrive all over the world. The generally exclusive mystery schools, notwithstanding their great merit, do not indicate any significant worldwide spread of his brand of 'religiousness' to the mainstream. Nor do the orthodox religions unanimously consider his teachings a particular threat.

SWAMI SATAYA SAI BABA (1925–)
Siddhi Yogi

This man proclaims himself the reincarnation of the Muslim mystic Sai Baba (1856–1916). He is a noted miracle worker, with millions of disciples in India and a more modest following in the West. In the Hindu tradition of sanyasi (seeker and follower) he wears orange robes and, currently, shows little interest in travelling to the West. His teachings are primarily Hindu-fundamentalist mainstream. There is no Hermetic aspect to his work (see Clue 2). Of the living masters, Satya Sai Baba has one of the largest followings, but his movement is confined mainly to India. Though his teachings do not constitute any threat to international authorities, an assassination attempt was made on his life in June 1993 by former disciples with connections to extreme Hindu fundamentalist groups. Since 1986, no significant change in his status has taken place, and there are signs that outside India his movement is gradually losing momentum.

SUN MYUNG MOON (1920 –)
Founder of Unification Church

Sun Myung Moon's Church has come into conflict with the authorities on numerous occasions and, as a result, Moon has spent a period in jail. With a linguistic stretch, his last name phonetically at least coincides with Nostradamus' prediction that the leader will be associated with the moon, *la lune* (see Clue 6) – that is, if Nostradamus was playing around with French words hiding English meanings. Moon has antagonized many people with his claim that he is the Christ of the Second Coming prophecies of the Christian Bible. He has also angered families and members of the public by the apparent disruption that adherence to his Church causes in the family lives of his followers. He has travelled extensively and his symbol is a red rising sun in the east. He is an arch anti-communist (*delivering the people of the world from slavery* [see Clue 5]).

Since my first book on Nostradamus (1986) Moon, now released from jail, has gone significantly mainstream in the right-wing Christian fundamentalist movement in the American Republican Party. Mainstream evangelist leaders such as Jerry Falwell embraced him. Evidence supports the contention that Moon's Unification Church has been a major financial supporter of former presidents Reagan and George Bush, Sr. Though Moon resembles more Nostradamian clues than any other teacher examined thus far, he appears to be turning into a politically correct religious insider rather than a spiritual rebel. No connections with Hermes (Clue 2) are evident. Claiming himself to be the messianic successor to the founder of one of the major orthodox religions does not make him the foretold catalyst of a new religion. The Man from the East will not come to renew the 'rocks' of an old dogma; he comes to destroy and replace them altogether with a new religion.

Adi Da Santosha (1939–)
American mystic

Adi Da Santosha (previously known as Bubba and Da Free John) continues to draw a growing following. Currently resident in the Fiji Islands, this unpredictable American mystic calls himself a Master of the Heart. He teaches self-transcendence or union with God, otherwise known as Divine Consciousness. This is a Hermetic teaching that works through self-observation of each moment – 'now' (see Clue 8). Adi Da has suffered considerable persecution from organized religions and governments.

Adi Da is not from the East (see Clue 1), although he was a disciple of masters in India and his teachings have Eastern origins. He does, however, make the controversial claim to be the reincarnation of the 19th-century Indian swami, Vivekananda (1863–1902), who could be called one of the first mystical trailblazers 'from the East' bringing Eastern teachings to Europe and America. Corporeal conundrums aside, Adi Da has travelled extensively and lived in India as a disciple before his self-realization. His teachings are unquestionably related to the Eastern flame (see Clue 4) and the symbolic Martian *red* (see *Epistle* quote – Clue 5). No significant relationship exists to *birds*: the Free Diast movement uses as its symbol the Dawn Horse, a prehistoric variant of Kalki, the White Horse of Hindu prophetic tradition that signifies Adi Da's claim to be the tenth and final Avatar (Messiah) of the Hindu prophetic tradition.

The mid-1990s saw another transformation of Adi Da's name and teaching style; yet the scope of his movement is limited compared with the burgeoning increase in the followings of Maharishi Mahesh Yogi or Osho.

SWAMI MAHARISHI MAHESH YOGI (1911–)
Founder of the Transcendental Meditation Movement (TM)

A former physicist, born in northern India, this leader founded the highly successful TM Movement, now practised by millions in the West as a technique for personal stress reduction and the attainment of inner tranquility. He has also travelled widely and provoked considerable controversy, especially during the 1960s when he became the 'guru' of the Beatles rock and roll group. TM has taproots in the ancient Hindu Vedic Scriptures and seems now to have been largely accepted by orthodox religions as representative of the New Age movements. It was taught in Western colleges until 1977.

The Maharishi and the TM movement have survived to see the new millennium; however, the Maharishi's generally diplomatic integration with the religious mainstream does not bode well for fulfilling Nostradamus' forecast of the new world teacher from the East being one who will shake down the dogmas of fossilized religious thought.

OSHO (1931–90)
(FORMERLY KNOWN AS BHAGWAN SHREE RAJNEESH)
Indian philosopher

A former philosophy professor from India, this man and his following was front-page news all over the world during the 1980s. His red-clad followers, called Neo-Sannyasins, have taken part in his experimental communes in India, Europe and the United States, and political, local and religious controversy surrounds him and his memory even into the new millennium. Osho's spontaneous daily discourses on love and meditation embraced a wide range of subjects, from sex to superconsciousness. His merciless, humour-filled insights into man's unconscious and conditioned behaviour, and his uncompromising, critical view of political and religious institutions as a mafia of the soul have earned him unanimous rejection by all mainstream religions. In the mid-eighties, Osho was jailed and deported from the United States. After his departure, his attempt to go on a world religious tour met with strong political and theological pressure and he was expelled from or denied entry to 21 countries in the space of only five months.

His followers allege that pressure from the Christian-fundamentalist-controlled Reagan government used threats to pressure other governments to keep their borders closed to the mystic. An example of this is detailed in investigative reporter Max Brecher's book

A Passage to America. Osho was one step away from being granted permanent residency in Uruguay when, according to Brecher's highly placed sources, the Uruguayan president Sanguinetti received a phone call from the American Ambassador Malcolm Wilkey, who said: 'You are a free country. You can do what you want. But you owe the United States six billion dollars. And this is the year for renegotiating a new loan. If you do not make your payments on time, we will raise the interest rates.'

Sanguinetti discovered that the thinly veiled threat hinged on Uruguay granting Osho permanent residency. The Uruguayan government decided not to grant permanent residency to the mystic and he was very pressingly 'invited to leave'. Not long afterwards Sanguinetti was invited to the Reagan White House, where it was announced that Uruguay's loan would be, after all, extended, and that his country would be the location for the next round of GATT (General Agreement on Tariffs and Trade) talks.

In 1986, the movement reestablished itself in Poona, India. Osho died of heart failure in early 1990. His followers claim that he died from complications from being poisoned by the US government while he was in prison in the El Reno Penitentiary in Oklahoma in November 1985. No clear evidence of poisoning was found by doctors who examined him prior to his death, although it is a known fact that thallium is an assassination poison of choice of organizations like the CIA because symptoms of damage appear only after two years, by which time the poison itself cannot be found in the victim's body.

Osho is from the East (Clue 1), and his teachings lean towards Tantra, the Eastern religious discipline related to Western Hermetic teachings (Clue 2). Tantra also contains the meditative concept of living in the present – the *Now* (see Clue 8). The Osho movement was symbolized in the 1980s by two flying birds; its current symbol is a lone swan flying free from the bonds of Earth and into the cosmos (see Clue 8). Osho was an infuriating traveller (see Clue 7) to the status quo religions and was thrown out of 21 countries while on his world tour (see Clue 3).

Osho's full legal name – Rajneesh Chandra Mohan – has two connections with *Moon*. 'Rajneesh' means 'Lord of the Full Moon', and his mid or *second to last name*, 'Chandra', means 'Moon' (Clue 6).

Although his followers have ceased to wear their red colours in public, their main headquarters at an ashram in India teems with thousands of people wearing robes in shades of maroon (red/rose colour: Clues 4 and 5) and even taught them a meditation called 'the *Mystic Rose*' (Clue 4). Despite his death, Osho's movement continues to flourish: Erich Folath of *Stern* magazine reported in 1993 that attendance at Osho's commune was up by 40 per cent from the previous year. In 1995, their commune reported their biggest increase of attendance ever;

interestingly 60 per cent never knew the guru while he was alive. The new millennium sees a surprising upsurge in interest in Osho's books on meditation. Many of his titles are among the hottest sellers in over 30 nations. On average pilgrims from 110 countries visit his main meditation resort in Poona, India. Although new generations of seekers are swelling the numbers of the movement, it clearly has not obtained the level of religious tolerance and outright acceptance that most of the other candidates listed briefly here enjoy. The labels 'spiritual rebel' and even 'spiritual terrorist' remain associated with this most controversial of 20th-century mystics as his post-mortem legacy continues to 'infuriate' and 'unite' the religions of the world against him.

Osho's links to Nostradamus' eight provided clues seem to match extremely well. We do not know, of course, that the prophet intended his quatrains to imply one religious leader – there could be several: *Many rare birds will cry in the air. 'Now! Now!'*

Phœnix

CHAPTER III
PROPHECIES
FOR THE
FAR DISTANT
FUTURE

*

We now enter the fantastic and metaphorical off-world visions of Nostradamus. The light of distant future meaning gleaned from the crowded star field of his familiar phrases, and prophetic themes is faint. Indeed, in the following prophecies we may mistake the afterglow of something far more immediate and present day in his message, rather than catch the subtle glimmer of a distant quasar-like prophecy about millennia to come.

THEY WILL LIVE IN THE SKY, FREE FROM POLITICS

Si grand Famine par vnde peſtifere,
Par pluye longue le long du polle arctique:
Samarobryn cent lieux de l'hemiſphere,
Viuront ſans loy exempt de pollitique.

So great a famine through a pestilent wave.
[*It*] will extend its rain over the length of the Arctic pole:
Samarobrin, one hundred leagues from the hemisphere,
They shall live without law, exempt from politics.

(Century 6 : Quatrain 5)

The name *Samarobrin* has mystified interpreters of Nostradamus for centuries. According to the quatrain, whatever Samarobrin is, it is hovering some *hundred leagues* or 270 miles above us. Modern interpreters have come up with an intriguing interpretation for this mysterious word: in Russian, *SAMO* means 'self' and *ROBRIN* means 'operator'; hence, this often used term 'self-operator' by Russian cosmonauts for their space satellites could make Samarobrin stand for either the Russian space station *Mir* or today's International Space Station currently under construction. Perhaps Nostradamus, when faced with the images of a space station aloft over the limb of the earth, with solar wings outstretched, could describe it only in terms of the winged seed pods of elm or maple trees, which are called *Samara* in Latin. He then added the Latin *obire* to describe it 'orbiting' the Earth.

Samarobrin could be the source of a rare positive prediction from Nostradamus. This quatrain may imply that scientists aloft in the International Space Station, working in their zero-gravity space labs, may find a cure for AIDS or some other future pandemic ravaging the northern hemisphere of Earth. They create new elements in space that cannot be manufactured in gravity on Earth. These inventors shall live *exempt* (or better – *beyond*) mere national law and work to find global solutions 270 miles in orbit above the petty politics of our planet. Or, we can take a broader brush to the cryptic promises of this prophecy and say that space exploration in the 21st century will bring solutions and cures to many of our ills and pestilences, whether some third Antichrist triggers them or they arise from the culmination of our anti-conscious behaviour. A world seen ever more often from space has no borders and its people are one family.

Finally, Samarobrin could even be Nostradamus' name for an extraterrestrial space craft that orbits Earth in our near future and by its unquestionable existence brings humanity together. The discovery of intelligent life will force us to live intelligently, as such a craft would be proof that others are out there (be they good or evil in intent) and humanity will need to put up a wiser and united front to deal with them.

'PHONING HOME' FROM A DISTANT WORLD

La nef estrange par le tourment marin,
Abourdera pres de port incogneu:
Nonobstant fignes de rameau palmerin,
Apres mort pille bon auis tard venu.

Because of the tormented seas, the strange ship
Will land at an unknown port:
Notwithstanding the signals from the branch of palm [*radar dish?*]
After death, pillage: good birds arriving late.

(Century 1 : Quatrain 30)

A strange and alien ship exits the ionic and radioactive solar gales of space to land at an unknown port – a new world. Are they humans come to colonize a new Earth under the stars of a new heaven mentioned later by Nostradamus as those seen from a planet within the constellations of Aquarius or Cancer? We do not know. A shaft extends from the vehicle that opens the palm-frond-like array of a communication dish, perhaps in the 30th year of the 21st or the 22nd century or perhaps a year 30 in a century far beyond the next turn of the millennium beyond 3001 A.D.

THE FIRST INTER-GALACTIC WAR?

Les dieux feront aux humains apparence,
Ce qu'ilz feront auteurs de grand conflict:
Auant ciel veu ferain espee & lance,
Que vers main gauche fera plus grand afflict.

The Gods will make it appear to the humans,
That they will be the authors of a great conflict:
Sword and lance [–*like missiles fly*]
before heaven [*which*] is observed as serene,
So that towards the left hand there will be great affliction.

(Century 1 : Quatrain 91)

The next great age of warfare could come on the battlefield of the stars. The gods could be an advanced human or alien race responsible for a war in the serene and silent heaven called 'Space'. These Gods may try to hide their responsibility for starting this conflict. Have they hidden the seed of a future showdown in the genetic double helix of the humans they interbred with eons ago? For a million years, the seed of conflict waited, until the day when humans freed themselves from the tether of their little world and entered the vast galactic arena. They contact the 'gods' responsible for the theological and mythological fragments that are the foundation of human religions and find the original characters of their myths and scriptures far too frail and human like themselves to regard with awe and fear. Indeed, the humans coming this far from deep space to confront their ancestors have become godlike in their own right. Conflict is joined. There is a new battle in heaven between angels. The new human, space-faring gods of the future crowd their ancestors off the galactic plane.

GENETICALLY TAILORED 'AQUA-HUMANS'

Au Cruftamin par mer Hadriatique,
Apparoiftra vn horrible poiffon:
De face humaine & la fin aquatique,
Qui fe prendra dehors de l'ameçon.

In the Conca by the Adriatic Sea,
There will appear a horrible fish:
With a face [*that is*] human and its end aquatic,
Which will be taken without the hook.

(Century 3 : Quatrain 21)

The Conca River drains into the Adriatic ten miles south of Rimini, the site of Nostradamus' first vision of the coming human era of multiple species. Enjoy the good old days of a single human species, for this new 21st century will be the last century to see it. Once human beings get over their fears of playing god with genetic engineering, once they begin adapting to the different gravities and atmospheres of other worlds in the solar system, and grapple with life in the weightlessness of space, you will see *Homo sapiens* branch off into many different species of human. By the 22nd century, you will think we have fashioned out of the root *Homo sapiens* species as many variants as earlier geneticists fashioned from breeding thousands of canine 'woof' creations from the mother 'wolf'. We will spawn as many variations of the human species tomorrow as we fashion variations of cat and dog today. In this prophecy, Nostradamus may describe the human face of a flippered and scale-skinned man or woman tailored for life beneath the sea.

A COSMIC CHRIST IS COMING

Le facree pompe viendra baiffer les aifles,
Par la venue du grand legiflateur:
Humble haulfera vexera les rebelles,
Naiftra sur terre aucun œmulateur.

The sacred pomp will come to lower its wings,
At the coming of the great legislator:
He will raise the humble. He will vex the rebels,
None of his like will be born on this earth.

(Century 5 : Quatrain 79)

A distant future interpretation would have this *legislator* be a human born in space or on an extra-planetary colony in our solar system, or a visitor from another star system. Perhaps the one who legislates is the great Messiah of the Aquarian Age, born in the 25th century, as foreseen by the British palmist and seer Count Louis Hamon in his book *Cheiro's World Predictions* (1931).

HOMO ANGELICUS

Le regne humain d'Anglique geniture,
Fera son regne paix vnion tenir:
Captiue guerre demy de sa closture,
Long temps la paix leur fera maintenir.

The human realm of Angelic offspring,
Will cause its [*his*] realm to hold in peace and union:
War captive halfway inside its [*his*] enclosure,
For a long time peace will be maintained by them.

(Century 10 : Quatrain 42)

Space-faring humanity will genetically bond with an extraterrestrial humanoid race to take on an appearance that our 16th-century prophet can describe only as *angelic* in appearance and nature. This union will eventually bring a lasting peace on Earth – and any new Earths colonized by our distant descendants.

3797 A.D.
THE END OF THE WORLD
AND A NEW BEGINING

...I'ay composéliures de propheties contenāt chacun

cent quatrains aftronomiques de propheties, lefquelles

i'ay vn peu voulu rabouter obfcurement: & font

perpetuelles vaticinations, pour d'icy à l'annee 3797.

...Que ie treuue le mõde auãt l'vniuerfelle cõflagration

aduenir tant de deluges & fi hautes inundations,

qu'il ne fera guiere terroir qui ne foit

couuert d'eau & fera par fi longtemps que hors mis

enographies & topographies, que le tout ne foit

pery: außi auāt & apres telles inundatiōs, en

plufieurs cōtrees, les pluyes feront fi exigues,

& tōbera du Ciel fi grande abondāce de feu & de

pierre candentes, que n'y demeurera rien qu'il ne

foit cōfommé: & cecy aduenir en brief, & auāt la

derniere conflagration. Car encores que la planette,

Mars paracheue fon fiecle, & à la fin de fon

dernier periode fi le reprendra il: mais affemblez

les vns en Aquarius par plufieurs annees,

les autres en Cancer par plus longues & cōtinues.

[From the Preface to the Prophecies of Nostradamus]

243

...I have composed books of prophecies, each containing one hundred astronomical quatrains composed of prophecies, which I have required to polish a little obscurely. They are perpetual prophecies, for they extend from now to the year 3797...

...Before the future universal conflagration [*in 3797*] the world will see many floods and such high inundations, that there will remain scarcely any land not covered by water, and this will last for so long that outside of the topography of earth – and the races which inhabit it – everything will perish. Furthermore, before and after these floods many nations shall see very little rain and there will fall from the sky such a great amount of fire and flaming meteors that nothing will remain unconsumed. All this will happen a short time before the final conflagration. For although the planet Mars will finish its cycle, at the end of its last age, it will start again: some will assemble in Aquarius for several years, others in Cancer for a longer time and for evermore.

[From the Preface to the Prophecies of Nostradamus]

The date 3797 makes this the most distant dated prediction in history. Nostradamus foresees tremendous gravitational disturbances of a dying Sun making Earth's climate go haywire. These are the first symptoms of the end of the world. Great tidal waves taller than continents will roll over Earth's antiquities and ancient-future civilizations. Then a meteor shower of debris from the remains of Venus and Mercury – as the expanding Sun captures them – reduces the surface of our planet to a scorched wasteland. The oceans evaporate and our home planet is consumed.

Astronomers say that the Earth will survive being overcome by the expanding Sun. It will orbit as a white-hot rock in the flames of a red giant (what Nostradamus calls *the final conflagration*). Nostradamus' belief that Mars would continue its orbit outside the Sun might find grudging agreement among astronomers. They believe the ageing Sun will have enough mass to expand at – or slightly beyond – the Earth's orbit when it swells into a red giant. Nostradamus and modern astronomers differ on the timing of cosmic doomsday. He believed this would occur 1,797 years after the year 2000. They see it several billion years later.

Even among the embers of this last conflagration the human race will survive to colonize space. Nostradamus not only reports on the survival of Mars but uses its astrological cycle to define a window of time. In Julian calculation an era of Mars lasts roughly

700 years. With this in mind he is possibly dating the period it takes a number of 'arcs' to travel the great distances of the galaxy to colonize other star systems. Tonight, when you step out of your home to behold the vault of the heavens, train your eye upon the distant stars of the constellations of Aquarius and Cancer. There you will see humanity's future home when your descendants will walk upon a new Earth warmed by the sunlight of distant stars. Nostradamus gives some indication that the mission to the stars of Cancer will see humankind build its permanent home. The Old French meaning for *cõtinues* (an abbreviation for *continues* in Modern French) gives us 'uninterrupted' or *evermore*. Another translation would

have our descendants dwelling in worlds around the stars of Cancer *for a longer and uninterrupted time.* Perhaps they will live consciously celebrating the eternity of the present, and therefore live beyond the interruptions of time itself.

Epilogue:
Scared Straight

✳

These visions of space travel, lived in peace and perpetuity – and other prescient promises of the coming of a new religiousness spawned by the appearance of a 'Man from the East' – appear in this book with an impact way out of proportion to the general tone of Nostradamus' discourse on the future. Taken in its totality, his tone is the most pessimistic and dark of any prophet who ever lifted the veil of tomorrow. It is an account of murder, tragedy and violent revolutions – even the Bible has one Antichrist, but Nostradamus burdens us with three. If positive futures appear, they seem to do so grudgingly. You can see this fact evident in the quatrain indexing for the Man from the East predictions. They are scattered like lotuses on the muddy floodwaters of ominous auguries of slaughter and sorrows.

Nostradamus nags us about our faults in future tense. It is a shrewish wife's litany of how often we have, and will, miss our chances to be anything more than robotic, predictable, murderous animals that talk of peace and enlightenment while walking the path of savagery and stupidity.

An Edgar Cayce will sleep-trance his nightmares to us of vast natural disasters and the sinking and rising of continents, but he always balances them with soft and assuring dreams of a Christ-consciousness-driven new humanity to come. Ruth Montgomery's guides frighten us with Axis Shift prophecies set for the end of the 20th century, but at least they take pity on us when the deadline of doom comes near and toss us another timeline of a decade's length. I would add that her spirit guides will be kind enough to keep postponing the tilt of the earth, with its subsequent thousand-mile winds and thousand-foot waves destroying civilization, ever to the next decade, and the next, until that eventuality is thrown in the refuse bin of 'never-to-happen' where it always belonged. The politically correct prophets will always positively promise a sun-shiny day after the end of days. Not

Nostradamus. He seems predisposed to view the world as a seer of sour grapes. His vision of the future is almost criminal. And that, dear reader, may be why his view of the future is far more profound than that of any other seer.

Who else but a criminal can teach you a lesson of hard love?

I saw such a lesson given once in an award-winning American television documentary entitled *Scared Straight*. It concerned a group of American teenage toughs who, upon facing the judge for their petty crimes, were given the choice of going to juvenile jail, or spending an afternoon in the State Penitentiary in an encounter session with a dozen of its worst convicts. In short, the judge was giving these delinquents a chance to see and change their future lives, if they but listen to the forecasts and confessions of the lifers – the men living in the seventh hell of prison for life.

Guards led the young toughs into the dark and barred halls of the penitentiary through a gauntlet of cat-calling, lewd and violent prisoners to sit in a room with the meanest, muscled, scar-faced men in perpetual life-lockdown. The 'session' began. An hour later, the cool, tough punks exited the room tearful and vulnerable boys. Eighty per cent of those boys would never commit a crime again. The transformation came from just one hour sitting face to face with their future. The convicts had become their Nostradamus, depicting without pity the horrors of what they could expect from a future prison life. There was no let-up to the auguries. They heard of assured rape of pretty young new prisoners, the mutilation of body and the deeper mutilation to the soul to come from the brutality of day to day existence spent for the rest of one's life in prison.

Every time I enter the prophecies of Nostradamus I feel like those boys encountering a man, who out of hard love has seen and understood what is potentially criminal in me, and in you: the destiny of being predictable makes us all passive or active participants in the repeated tragedy of history Nostradamus foretells. The prophet, like the convicts of that prison, does not pull his punches. He rarely gives us hope. His words are full of frightening and violent images of what we have done and 'will' do if we remain hell-bent on perpetuating the fundamental crime of every human being. That crime is this: being programmed by society from birth onwards to be predictable, robotic, a dutiful mediocrity and a collector of borrowed personal, national and religious identities. When we are not living from our own truth and experiences, when we allow others to suppress the birthright of natural intelligence and Christ-consciousness in us, then we become delinquent as spiritual beings. Rather than face life with the spontaneity of genius and authenticity we as children are forced to follow the paths of the adults who overlord and overwhelm us early on. They do this because the crime was 'done' to them. The victims of this criminal conditioning pass it on to the young of our world, just as old prisoners pass on their criminal skills to the new inmates of their world.

I believe Nostradamus saw this repetition of habit as the engine of all that is horrible in our future history. He has applied that pessimism to extremes out of compassion. He is trying to scare us straight. He used fire to put out fire, as it were. Rather than give us condolences and hope, he scares us with the crimes of the future, the wars and the devastations. By painting a future so dire he is like those brutal convicts breathing down on our delinquent dreams that all will turn out good in the end because someone else – not you or me – will wake up in time and change the future's course for the better. You can hold that idea, and think you are pretty cool and aware until you enter his prophecies and see him rave and rant therein. You will soon find out that you and your future are not that cool, and you know nothing about being tough. You will see from his litany of prophecies fulfilled and prophecies to come that you are part of the crime of habit that plants seeds of tomorrow's wars and tragedies in every new generation. You are today's criminal teaching your children to be criminals tomorrow and Nostradamus, a prisoner of pessimistic prophecy for life, is trying to scare you straight out of that habit.

Once you come out of his chamber of horrors into the sunlight, take his lesson to heart and to soul. *Change.*

Phœnix

FURTHER READING

FURTHER READING

This booklet is little more than a glimpse of what is possible in the future according to Nostradamus. To gain a more comprehensive understanding of my interpretation of his prophecies please read the following:

NOSTRADAMUS:
THE NEW MILLENNIUM
(Element, 2001)

NOSTRADAMUS:
THE COMPLETE PROPHECIES
(Element, 1997)

To gain a better understanding of how I compare Nostradamus' prophecies to other traditions please read the following:

MESSIAHS:
The Visions and Prophecies for the Second Coming
(Element, 1999)

1000 FOR 2000:
Startling Predictions for the New Millennium
from Prophets Ancient and Modern
(HarperSanFrancisco, 1999)

THE LAST POPE:
The Decline and Fall of the Church of Rome *(Element, 1998)*

THE MILLENNIUM BOOK OF PROPHECY:
777 Visions and Predictions from Nostradamus, Edgar Cayce,
Gurdjieff, Tamo-san, Madame Blavatsky, Old and New
Testament Prophets, and 89 Others
(Harper San Francisco, 1997)

CONTACT ADDRESSES

My work generates many questions and comments from my readers. The best way to contact me is through email. By emailing your comments and questions my response time is within a month. If you write to me by regular mail it could take years. I hope to hear from you soon.

Web site: www.hogueprophecy.com

Email address: talktome@hogueprophecy.com

PICTURE CREDITS

The publisher wishes to thank the Corbis picture agency
for the images on the following pages:

Frontispiece: © CORBIS

Page 26-27: © Bettmann/CORBIS

Page 42-43: © Bettmann/CORBIS

Page 70-71: © Leonard de Selva/CORBIS

Page 80-81: © Hulton-Deutsch Collection/CORBIS

Page 88-89: © Bettmann/CORBIS

Page 100-101: © Bettmann/CORBIS

Page 114-115: © ANDY LEVIN/CORBIS SYGMA

Page 138-139: © Bettmann/CORBIS

Phœnix

INDEX